The Revd Dr Steven Shakespeare is the Anglican Chaplain at Liverpool Hope University, UK. He studied theology at the University of Cambridge, where he completed his PhD on the Danish philosopher Søren Kierkegaard. He is the author of *Kierkegaard, Language and the Reality of God* (Ashgate 2001) and co-author (with Hugh Rayment-Pickard) of *The Inclusive God: Reclaiming Theology for an Inclusive Church* (Canterbury Press 2006).

RADICAL ORTHODOXY

A critical introduction

STEVEN SHAKESPEARE

First published in Great Britain in 2007

Society for Promoting Christian Knowledge
36 Causton Street
London SW1P 4ST

British Library Cataloguing-in-Publication Data
A catalogue record for this book is available from the British Library

ISBN 978–0–281–05837–2

1 3 5 7 9 10 8 6 4 2

Typeset by Graphicraft Ltd, Hong Kong
Printed in Great Britain by Ashford Colour Press

Produced on paper from sustainable forests

Contents

Contents

Acknowledgements

I am grateful to friends and colleagues with whom I have discussed many of the issues in this book (when they were probably desperate to talk about something else!). Among them are Matt Thompson, Will Lamb, Hugh Rayment-Pickard, Gerard Mannion, Don Cupitt and George Pattison.

My thanks also go to Rebecca Mulhearn at SPCK for commissioning the project, helping to clarify its focus and bearing with my delays. Liverpool Hope University provided an understanding setting in which I could combine research and writing with my real job.

Finally, I would like to thank Sally who supported me through the writing process, and all the wonderful mood swings that accompanied it.

Abbreviations

The main works referred to in the text are cited using the abbreviations in this list. Details of other works can be found in the Notes. A selection of further reading appears at the end of the book.

AW   Catherine Pickstock, *After Writing: On the Liturgical Consummation of Philosophy*, Blackwell, Oxford, 1998.

BR   John Milbank, *Being Reconciled: Ontology and Pardon*, Routledge, London, 2003.

CG   Graham Ward, *Cities of God*, Routledge, London, 2000.

CTRP   Graham Ward, *Cultural Transformation and Religious Practice*, Cambridge University Press, Cambridge, 2005.

DE   Stephen Long, *Divine Economy: Theology and the Market*, Routledge, London, 2000.

DRO   Wayne Hankey and Douglas Hedley (eds), *Deconstructing Radical Orthodoxy: Postmodern Theology, Rhetoric and Truth*, Ashgate, Aldershot, 2005.

ED   John Milbank, 'The End of Dialogue' in Gavin D'Costa (ed.), *Christian Uniqueness Reconsidered: The Myth of a Pluralistic Theology of Religions*, Orbis Books, Maryknoll, 1990, pp. 174–91.

ITP   Rosemary Radford Ruether and Marion Grau (eds), *Interpreting the Postmodern: Responses to 'Radical Orthodoxy'*, T & T Clark, New York and London, 2006.

LTEH   Daniel Bell, *Liberation Theology after the End of History: The Refusal to Cease Suffering*, Routledge, London, 2001.

PSP   Philip Blond (ed.), *Post-Secular Philosophy: Between Philosophy and Theology*, Routledge, London, 1998.

ROCE   Laurence Hemming (ed.), *Radical Orthodoxy? A Catholic Enquiry*, Ashgate, Aldershot, 2000.

Abbreviations

RONT John Milbank, Catherine Pickstock and Graham Ward (eds), *Radical Orthodoxy: A New Theology*, Routledge, London, 1999.

RORT James K. A. Smith and James H. Olthius (eds), *Radical Orthodoxy and the Reformed Tradition: Creation, Covenant and Participation*, Baker Academic, Grand Rapids, 2005.

ST James K. A. Smith, *Speech and Theology: The Language and Logic of Incarnation*, Routledge, London, 2002.

TA John Milbank and Catherine Pickstock, *Truth in Aquinas*, Routledge, London, 2001.

TST John Milbank, *Theology and Social Theory: Beyond Secular Reason*, Blackwell, Oxford, 1990.

TST(2) John Milbank, *Theology and Social Theory: Beyond Secular Reason*, Blackwell, Oxford, 2nd edition, 2006.

WMS John Milbank, *The Word Made Strange: Theology, Language, Culture*, Blackwell, Oxford, 1997.

Introduction: insider theology?

In the spoof 'rockumentary' *This is Spinal Tap* (1984), we join the ageing heavy metal band of the film's title as they make their way towards the stage at a Cleveland concert venue. Unfortunately, the trip from the dressing room to the limelight passes through a maze of subterranean corridors. The band members find themselves completely lost, walking round and round in circles looking for a door that says 'Authorized Personnel Only'. A helpful maintenance man only succeeds in confusing them even more with his directions. All the time we can hear the crowd chanting, but the lead singer's cry of 'Hello Cleveland!' only echoes in the bowels of the underground labyrinth.

For some contemporary theologians, this story offers a good reflection of the dominant ways of thinking in the modern world. They argue that modern, secular thought and culture is trapped in a maze. It dreams of a future of freedom, truth and fulfilment. But it has cut itself off from the only real way to make that dream a reality.

Secular thought imagines a world without God, a world without a genuine relationship to what transcends it. And without that relationship, it is doomed to the life of a laboratory rat, scuttling through an endless one-dimensional maze. For all the variety of turnings and surroundings it moves through, the rat only ever encounters variations on the same old thing. When passageways don't really go anywhere, one is as good as another. Nothing new, nothing different, nothing world-changing can ever happen. There is no end, no purpose, no way out.

For the theologians we will examine in this book, this is the sickness of the modern world. Radical Orthodoxy sets out to show how that sickness can only be overcome by a theology and a Church that claims the authority to open different levels of reality, and tell a different story of how things are with us. They make the bold assertion that only by telling the Christian story can we rediscover our true end. And only within the Church can this story effectively shape people to live lives that embody the truth.

These bold claims have attracted their share of criticism, as we shall see. A repeated objection has been that this type of theology only succeeds in catching us in a new trap. It turns the Church in on itself, pits the Christian community against all others. For some critics, this is a dangerous path to go down. It can mean the Church gets stuck in a ghetto, its own maze. The Church risks becoming entirely cut off from all other voices, or sources of truth, or experiences of God.

So which is it? Is it modernity which is lost and trapped as it desperately seeks an exit from its troubles? Or is it the Church which has separated itself from where the real light and life are?

Of course, either-ors like this usually turn out to be much too simplistic. What matters is that we take the issues seriously. Fudge is sweet, but it makes bad theology. The writers we will be looking at are clear that these are issues about real life and death, about what matters and how we can live in a way that doesn't give the last word to violence, competition, domination and superficial consumerism. They demand our attention and our commitment.

Before we plunge into the waters, however, I have to acknowledge a problem from the outset. Over the course of writing this book, whenever people have asked me what I am working on, I have watched their reaction to the answer. As soon as I mention 'Radical Orthodoxy' or 'postliberalism' I see eyes glaze over or else narrow in horror. It has given me a new appreciation of what it was like for my wife when she studied mathematics at postgraduate level. People would almost physically recoil when they heard what she did. Maths was alien and baffling to them, and some people seemed virtually afraid of it (they cheered up when she told them she was using it to study volcanic eruptions, but that's another story).

There is no doubt that Radical Orthodoxy has a fearsome and off-putting reputation for complexity. 'I don't understand all that,' I was told on more than one occasion by theologically educated people in full-time Christian ministry. The reputation,

it has to be said, is too often deserved. Books of radically orthodox theology are full of complex, detailed arguments about the
minutiae of texts and definitions, crammed with philosophical
jargon in a range of languages and laden with grand claims
which sound incredibly important if only one could work out
what they meant. As Stephen Long remarks, 'Radical orthodoxy's
labyrinthine prose tempts some to read it only as an academic
parlour game used for inconsequential power struggles in high-
brow university religion and philosophy departments.'[1] And that's
from someone who supports it!

However, it would be a pity if this were the final word, because the issues raised in this theology are crucial ones. They are
about the kind of world we now live in, and the powerful stories
which dominate it. They challenge those in the churches to ask:
can the Christian story still be told and heard? Is it just one
among many competing alternatives? Does it have a distinctive
voice and form? What kind of community, what sort of values
does it call into being? What does it say about economics, sex,
shopping, art, politics?

The theologians we will examine offer a vision of Christianity
which is provocative, engaged and unapologetic. They want to put
the Christian story back at the heart of our churches and their
witness to the world. For too long, they argue, the churches have
adopted the stories and values of the society around them,
putting a Christian gloss on them which does not disguise the truth
that they are in fact alien to and destructive of the gospel.

This trend in theology is exciting, sometimes baffling and
always controversial. It exploded on the theological scene, first
with John Milbank's epic *Theology and Social Theory*, in 1990.
It gathered momentum over the decade, and especially with the
publication of the collection of essays *Radical Orthodoxy: A
New Theology* in 1999, the first title in the 'Radical Orthodoxy'
series. A huge literature now exists, including special editions
of journals, the results of ecumenical conferences, and critical
responses. In the process, Radical Orthodoxy has not only had
a major academic impact (especially in the UK and USA), it has
also captured the imagination of many bright ordinands and

seminarians. It is therefore a significant factor in how many Christian thinkers and future leaders are addressing the place of theology and the Church in the twenty-first century.

Unfortunately, because it has been shaped by highly complex philosophical issues, it is often ignored or avoided by many in the churches (and even in theology faculties). This book is intended as something of a 'guide to the perplexed', helping students, clergy and indeed anyone with an interest in theology to engage with the debates.

Before spelling this out, however, it is worth saying what this book is not. It is not a comprehensive history or survey of Radical Orthodoxy. It does not seek to reference every book and article, track down every influence or cover every issue that these writers raise. Instead, my aim will be to identify, explain and question the main themes of this theology for those who are quite capable of wrestling with the ideas, but do not have the time or specialist knowledge to wade through a mass of publications and worthy commentary. In the process, I will try to make complex thought accessible without dumbing it down or evading tough issues.

The focus will be upon the three founding figures of the movement: John Milbank, first and foremost, but also Catherine Pickstock and Graham Ward. We will also be concentrating upon some of the other important volumes in the 'Radical Orthodoxy' series. Other books will be cited, but only because they might offer additional clarification or criticism. Although Radical Orthodoxy is not monolithic, keeping a core number of texts at the centre of our view will help in identifying its overall shape.

One thing has become clear: Radical Orthodoxy has touched a nerve. It can be bossy, infuriating, difficult and audacious. But it cannot be ignored.

A new theology?

The rest of this introduction prepares the way for more detailed analysis of the movement in later chapters. For ease of navigation, it is divided into the following headings:

1   *Diagnosing our sickness.* Radical Orthodoxy offers a therapy for the current ills of the modern, secularized world. This section will explore why its writers have such a problem with secular ways of thinking, both in society and in the Church. It will explain why Radical Orthodoxy is so insistent that Christian theology must be restored to its place as 'Queen of the Sciences', exposing the emptiness and violence which lurk behind the facade of contemporary liberal tolerance and universalism, as well as many of the varieties of 'postmodern' thought. And we will see why it is claimed that the roots of this sickness lie in heresy, in a theology deformed and disfigured by its loss of key Christian themes.

2   *Exposing quack medicine.* Radical Orthodoxy also has some cutting things to say about Christian responses to the modern world which it thinks are infected by secular ideas. We will get a better understanding of how the movement positions itself as we explore some of its disputes with Christian liberalism and conservatism, and its criticisms of liberation and ecological theology. In each case, we will see how Radical Orthodoxy accuses its opponents of separating some part of the world or human experience from God, and trying to use it as a neutral ground on which to start doing theology. Radical Orthodoxy is clear: there can be no such no-man's-land. We have to start within the language and practices of Christian orthodoxy.

3   *The cure of souls.* We will begin to see the shape of the alternative vision which Radical Orthodoxy offers. It claims that the Church and its story comes first. There is no secular realm, set apart from God. This is where it parts company with all forms of modern liberalism. However, it also puts the themes of analogy, participation in the life of God and the Eucharist centre stage. This is a theology which seeks to redeem the created world, our bodies, our history, our language and our communities. The gospel of Radical Orthodoxy – its proclamation of the fullness of God's gift and the original peace of creation – needs to be understood if we are to appreciate its imaginative power as well as its intellectual credentials.

4 *Second opinions.* For all its claim to be a 'new theology', Radical Orthodoxy is well aware that it belongs to a tradition of Christian theology (and its Greek philosophical forebears). It often interprets that tradition and thinkers such as Plato, Aquinas and Augustine in dramatic and challenging ways. We will look also at the contemporary context which has shaped the way the movement reads its past. This context includes the earlier *nouvelle théologie* associated with Henri de Lubac, and the ongoing development of theology which seeks a way beyond liberalism. Finally, the movement's own development will be briefly traced.

These claims, disputes and themes will be explored more fully in the chapters to come, when we will also have the chance to present some of the key criticisms of this 'new theology'. Radical Orthodoxy has been nothing if not controversial, and we will be looking at some of the more robust objections that have been made to it. In the process, we will also be asking whether there are alternative theological approaches which can meet and answer the challenges laid down by John Milbank and his fellow travellers.

These controversies have often been conducted in a high academic tone. But the questions they struggle with go to the heart of the Church's future. Is there an authentic Christian voice, vision and body for us today? Just what form can Christian witness take in a pluralistic and fragmented world? Is there any way out of the maze of competing perspectives in which we feel trapped? In an age of resurgent religion and secular backlash, of globalization and fundamentalism, where is true peace to be found?

Diagnosing our sickness

'Once, there was no "secular"' (*TST*, p. 9).

These words occur near the beginning of John Milbank's *Theology and Social Theory*. In this terse sentence, we find some important clues to the nature of Radical Orthodoxy and the controversies it has spawned.

First, Milbank is clear that ideas have a history. They do not just drop down ready-made from a timeless world above. They are formed in the ebb and flow of historical, social and economic change. Just because something seems obvious or natural to us, does not mean that it would seem so to a person in another cultural context or another period of history. One thing Milbank wants to do is to tell the story of why certain ideas have taken hold and become dominant in our world today. By telling the story, he also shows it has a beginning, and can have an end. He clears a space in which another story can be told. 'Once upon a time . . .' is not merely the beginning of a fairy tale. It is a subversive act of positioning a story to show how limited and questionable it is. Stories, for Milbank, are invented.

Second, these words state one of Radical Orthodoxy's core convictions. The 'secular' – which in the Western European tradition is the world interpreted as separate from the stories and practices of Christian faith – is not a given. It is not an objective fact, which is there whether we acknowledge it or not, waiting to be discovered. The secular is not the equivalent of Antarctica. It is more like the land reclaimed from the sea around the Netherlands. It is a human creation.

This has a further consequence. Human beings create things for reasons. Those reasons may be related to survival, power, usefulness, pleasure, and so on. In other words, creation is not a neutral act. The fashioning of the idea of the secular is no different. Milbank spends a great deal of time trying to convince us that it has been created to serve human interests, interests which have more do to with conquest and domination than reason and tolerance.

Third, the fallout from accepting that the secular has been made up also challenges Christian theology. On the one hand, it becomes impossible to cosy up to secular ideas and processes, and accept them as some sort of inevitable setting within which Christianity has to make its way. This, for Milbank, is the error of liberal theology and all that has flowed from it. On the other hand, however, the road taken by some more conservative modern theologies is no better. They try to speak from the mountain top, looking down on the evil secular world from a position of certainty. They try to exempt the Bible, or the teaching office of the Church from all the changes and chances of history. But Milbank thinks this is a false move. There is no jumping out of time and history. If we are to take on the secular and assert the superiority of Christianity, we can only do this by telling the Christian story (which includes Christian liturgy and action).

Conservative theologies are in fact just as much the children of modernity as liberal ones. This is because they still accept that there is a 'secular' world. They just view it differently from liberals, as a source of error and contamination. Their solution is to reach for a pure, eternal source of truth. But Radical Orthodoxy seeks to take our historical and cultural setting with utmost seriousness. Neither biblical fundamentalism nor the more extreme forms of Roman Catholic doctrines of papal and church authority can rescue us. They are too authoritarian, and they speak to the world from the 'outside'.

This turn away from conservative authoritarianism should not mislead us, however. Radical Orthodoxy is not a theology of compromise. It sets itself in opposition to the modern idea of the secular in no uncertain terms. How can it do this without playing the conservative card, however? To answer this question, we need to probe a little more deeply into why the secular is treated with such abhorrence.

According to John Milbank, 'The secular *episteme* is a post-Christian paganism, something in the last analysis only to be defined negatively, as a refusal of Christianity and the invention of an "Anti-Christianity"' (*TST*, p. 280). The word *episteme* comes from a Greek term which can often be translated simply as 'knowledge'. However, in this context Milbank is drawing on the way the word was used by the French philosopher Michel Foucault (1926–84).

Foucault was a genealogist of ideas. That's to say, he tried to show how key concepts and forms of thinking were born and shaped in very particular historical and cultural settings. Ideas such as 'madness' and 'perversion' were used to divide up and categorize the world in the interests of people who defined themselves as normal and sane. In Foucault's work, an *episteme* is not just a bit of knowledge, but the framework or system which tells us what counts as knowledge and what does not. For example, we might say that knowledge should be based on evidence. But under the surface of that statement are all sorts of hidden assumptions about what counts as evidence, and who decides what is valid and what is not.

So when Milbank refers to the secular *episteme*, he means something like this: the secular world is not value-neutral. It is not something that is based on pure, unbiased reason. In fact, it is a very prejudiced way of organizing our world and our thinking. It is full of undisclosed value judgements. Given the chance, it will impose its will upon us, and exclude all other ways of being in and valuing the world.

Secularization, then, is not merely a neutral, observable process in which beliefs and institutions based on faith or religious authority are supplanted by those based on science and reason alone. This is because the idea of the secular is itself based on a leap of faith. It is driven by the authoritative pronouncements of worldly powers who find it convenient to relegate religious claims to the private realm, where they cannot touch or question the modern capitalist way of organizing the world. As the introduction to *Radical Orthodoxy* states, 'For several centuries now, secularism has been defining and constructing the world. It is a world in which the theological is either discredited or turned into harmless leisure-time activity of private commitment' (*RONT*, p. 1).

Milbank's polemical claim follows on from this. Secular liberalism is not a scientifically based, objective view of the world. It is in fact an alternative religion. And it is a religion which cannot exist peacefully with Christianity, because it offers a fundamentally different vision of the world.

It is worth noting that Milbank associates secularism with paganism. Why? Because, for Milbank, paganism is ultimately about the worship of sheer power. It accepts the basic forces of the world as brute givens of fate, fortune and chance. The self-interest of nation states, the individual's drive for survival, the impersonal working of market forces – all of these are like the will of the gods in pre-Christian Greek myth. We can't live without them, but they are not directed towards any harmonious vision of the good, or any reconciliation of the different parts of our life. However much they are dressed up as something else, at bottom they are simply expressions of a blind will-to-power.

This secular religion of power-worship is not simply a modern invention, however. Augustine had already made a contrast between the earthly city (represented by the Roman Empire) whose peace is based on violent conquest, and the heavenly city, represented by the Church, which embodies a peace without violence. Perhaps more significant still for Radical Orthodoxy is the belief that the seeds of secular decadence are sown by developments within Christian theology itself.

The key villain of the piece is Duns Scotus, a medieval Franciscan theologian who died in the early fourteenth century. Scotus is accused of playing a major part in the breakdown of the 'analogical' world-view associated particularly with Thomas Aquinas (*c.* 1225–74). According to Aquinas, analogy was a way of talking about God which offered a middle way between two extremes. One extreme was univocal language, which assumed that words were used in exactly the same way when applied to God as they were when applied to anything else. This meant that God could only ever be different in degree (bigger and better) rather than different in kind from us and from the world. The other extreme was equivocal language, which held that words used of God meant something entirely different to their ordinary meaning. On this view, God was a blank, so utterly other to us that anything we said about God was empty and meaningless – hardly a promising prospect for religious practice!

Analogy tried to avoid these dead ends by saying that some language (like 'God is love' or 'God is truth') could be properly used of God, as God was the source and perfect end of such qualities. However, there was still a high degree of unknowing in this account, as we could not tell exactly *how* such words and expressions applied to God.

Ideas of analogy can be involved and sophisticated. But the important thing to hold on to is that they try to keep open a possibility for true speech about God which doesn't either reduce God to being just one more thing (however exalted) among many in the universe, or make God into a black hole eternally irrelevant to us.

Duns Scotus is blamed with distorting this authentically Christian understanding of God and truth, because he said that 'being' is a univocal concept. In other words, there is no difference between the way in which God 'is' and the way in which a person or anything else 'is'. To be is the same thing in each case. God is different from us because of the infinite nature of his power. But this has just the consequences which analogy tried to guard against. It makes God the same kind of being as us, just (infinitely) bigger and better. The irony is that Duns Scotus' univocal view doesn't make God any closer to us, because to preserve God's uniqueness, he has to emphasize God's exalted difference from all creatures. God becomes almost identified with pure power.

A further consequence is that, as God is no longer related to us by a living chain of analogy, God becomes ever more hidden and dark to us. God retreats into the heavens, exercising his will from afar. And God's will becomes the arbitrary exercise of power. It has no inner relationship to human worth and fulfilment. God becomes the Law, imposed upon an essentially godless world.

This account of Duns Scotus is highly controversial. Whether or not it is an accurate interpretation of his work, however, its role in Radical Orthodoxy's story of how we got where we are today is undeniable.[2] The conclusion offered is that the criticism of Christianity which gathers pace from the Enlightenment and into the nineteenth century is actually a development of Christian theology gone wrong. On the one hand, the idea of God is criticized by secularists for supporting arbitrary, oppressive power, and God is dismissed as the projection of our desire for power, or of our fear of a Father-figure. On the other hand, the retreat of God from the world creates an opportunity for the secular to assert its independence. The assumption is that we know what being is, independently of God. God becomes irrelevant, and other forces rush in to fill the gap. Unfortunately, these new forces are shaped in the image of the Power-God which they replace. A new cultural winter of militarism, imperialism and dictatorship is the result, all under the cover of increased enlightenment, civilization or socialism.

Theology and Social Theory uses this history as a starting point to critique the modern discipline of social science, which claims to give us objective facts about how society grows and works. Milbank counters:

> Secular 'scientific' understanding of society was, from the outset, only the self-knowledge of the self-construction of the secular as power. What theology has forgotten is that it cannot either contest or learn from this understanding as such, but has either to accept or deny its object. (*TST*, p. 10)

It's important to dwell on this point, because it underlines the dramatic nature of the claim that Radical Orthodoxy makes. Milbank is arguing that social science is anything but scientific, if by that we mean based on empirical evidence alone, and free of all ideological bias. In fact, social science exists only as the surface expression of a deeply questionable set of prejudices and ideas about value and truth. By bracketing out ideas of the transcendent, divine or supernatural, it presents us with a world that makes sense without any reference to the truth claims of theology or the reality of God's creative grace. But it can't do without some overriding order or principle in its view of the world. Something has to take the place of God, to ensure that this secular knowledge can have firm foundations. That 'something' can come in a variety of forms: in Darwinism and capitalist theory, it is the blind forces of nature, or self-interest, or the market; for progressives and socialists, it is the inevitable march of history towards civilization or revolution. In each case, what are supposed to be neutral 'facts' accessible to any reasonable observer, are revealed to be value judgements, asserted with all the dogmatism we might associate with religious fundamentalism. And, for Milbank, what each of these forces conceals is that, at bottom, they are founded on nothing other than the force of power and domination itself.

For Radical Orthodoxy, the Enlightenment dream of unbiased reason and universal values shelters a horrible violence in its heart. The age of progress coexists with European imperialism and racism, with concentration camps, gulags and genocide. Ward argues that 'there is no view from nowhere, no objective knowledge; the view from nowhere is itself a cultural ideology – often Western, white and male' (*CG*, p. 237). Nazi paganism and Stalinist 'scientific' socialism are only the most obvious examples of what happens when all value and truth are located in the power games of the world – consequences which also flow from the rich world's embrace of unfettered capitalism and its disregard for human worth. As Milbank writes, referring to the influential philosophy of Immanuel Kant, 'Kantian liberal humanist logic and Nazi logic are seamlessly linked, and Nazism was nothing but an unhindered attempt to raise man as a God, to unleash and perfect the power of human freedom' (*BR*, p. 179). He adds that 'the Holocaust was the supreme consummation of secularity' (*BR*, p. 180).

Ward, Pickstock and Milbank pronounce judgement upon this ideology in no uncertain terms:

> Today the logic of secularism is imploding. Speaking with a microphoned and digitally simulated voice, it proclaims – uneasily, or else increasingly unashamedly – its own lack of values and lack of meaning. In its cyberspaces and theme-parks it promotes a materialism which is soulless, aggressive, nonchalant and nihilistic. (*RONT*, p. 1)

Or, to quote Philip Blond:

> To say we should now bring an end to the secular is to say that we should reverse the dreadful consequences of the liberal erasure of

13

God and take myth out of the hands of the fascists where it has all too often fallen. (*PSP*, p. 54)

Take that, modernity.

Exposing quack medicine

The dire effects of the Enlightenment are not only felt outside Christian theology, however. Again and again, Radical Orthodox writers point to how Christian thinkers have allowed secular thought to set the agenda. As we have suggested, both liberals and conservatives are found guilty of fatal compromises with modernity. And the rot goes further. Liberation theology, for all it tries to fight the injustice of capitalism from the perspective of the poor, is charged with allowing too dominant a role to secular ideas of society, state and rights. Eco-theology, which seeks a more holistic understanding of the relationship between humanity, nature and God, is accused of turning nature into God. In each case, God is no longer allowed to be transcendent and other to the created world.

Already in *Theology and Social Reason*, Milbank takes up cudgels against the failings of liberation theology. He prepares for this by attacking the work of the Catholic theologian Karl Rahner (1904–84). Rahner's theology is associated with the re-forming tendencies of the Second Vatican Council of the Roman Catholic Church (1962–65), and the drive to be more open to the presence of God in the secular world and other faiths. Milbank summarizes Rahner's position as follows: 'there is no such thing as a state of "pure nature": rather, every person has always already been worked upon by grace' (*TST*, p. 206). Rahner believed that our humanity was, from its very roots, open to a transcendent dimension of being.

What is the problem with this? After all, it seems to chime in with Radical Orthodoxy's claim that there is no part of the world which can be understood in separation from God. However, according to Milbank, the way that Rahner and his followers follow up their insight actually undermines Christian claims.

The issue is this: how do we understand the relationship between nature and grace, between God and the world? Milbank describes two possible theological responses. One approach 'supernaturalizes the natural'. In other words, it gives first place to the way theology tells the story of the world as God's creation. The other response – and this is what Rahner is supposed to do – 'naturalizes the supernatural'. In its enthusiasm to bring harmony between nature and grace, it empties grace of all real content. Theology has nothing to say to the world, which is granted its own charter of independence. Rahner still tries to preserve a realm of nature apart from grace. The world has to be analysed by non-theological, non-Christian disciplines such as social science and psychology. Theology then comes along and adds a Christian gloss to the facts which these sciences uncover.

For Milbank, as we have seen, such an approach spells disaster for Christian theology, because the so-called scientific disciplines are exposed as anti-Christian systems of thought, laden with their own value judgements, their own distorted 'theology'. So Rahner's theology, far from leading to some kind of holistic vision, ends up by giving these atheistic and nihilistic philosophies the upper hand. Theology is pushed to the edges of the world.

Latin American liberation theology has been very critical of European liberalism, because the latter is blind to class conflict and the economic, structural injustices faced by the poor. However, according to Milbank, it still shares the failings of Rahner's liberal theology. It appeals to the social sciences, often to Marxism, as its source of truth about the world. Therefore, 'liberation theology is guilty, for all its protestations, of reducing the content of salvation to a quasi-Marxist concept of liberation' (*TST*, p. 235). Ironically, this liberation turns out to be a secular one, stripped of Christian content.

Following Milbank's lead, Daniel Bell and Stephen Long also write at length about the liberationist current in Christian theology. They agree with liberationists that capitalism is fundamentally at odds with Christianity. However, Bell argues that they still buy into the idea that the Church should be fighting for 'justice' as administered by the state. Contrary to appearances, they make the Church apolitical, surrendering its distinctiveness in the interests of abstract ideas of justice for all or human rights. The problem with these ideas is that they are not rooted in the specific stories and practices of the Christian faith. They are empty vessels, which can be manipulated by the powers that be. Liberation is thus made into a servant of that which it tries to oppose.

Bell claims that 'the Church is the exemplary human community' (*LTEH*, p. 72). This kind of claim – often made in Radical Orthodoxy – will be analysed in more detail later. For now, we simply need to get a flavour of what this means in practice. For Bell, it seems to imply a rejection of any alliance or compromise between the Church and civil society, those institutions which stand between the individual and the state. These institutions are fatally infected by capitalism and secularism:

> In this era of global capitalism, when Coca-Cola and Nike find their way into every nook and cranny of the earth well ahead of clean water, roads and life-sustaining diets, far from furthering the cause of liberation and life, civil society can only be a means of discipline, an instrument of the regnant capitalist order for overcoming resistance and forming desire in its own image.
>
> (*LTEH*, p. 70)

This is a bleak view indeed. The structure of the argument is all-encompassing. Everything that is not-Church is corrupted, for capitalism is a monster that devours everything in its path. It even thrives on dissent and revolution, turning them into yet more opportunities to create niche markets. Therefore, only an utterly different vision of the world, only a different politics wholly un-affected by worldly wisdom, can offer an alternative. And for Bell, this means the Church. Liberation theology makes some of the right noises, but by its sympathetic use of secular sociology and its alliances with wider civil movements, its betrays its own ends.

Such a seamless argument might begin to make us suspicious. Just what evidence is being called upon to support these universal claims? Can we really know in advance that all movements for political change outside the Church are merely the poodles of capitalist corporations? If capitalism is so devouring, how can we elevate the Church to a position of such superiority? If – as Bell admits – the Church itself can be compromised, where do we find the pure exemplary Church which is supposed to embody a different politics?

These questions also haunt Stephen Long's analysis of Christian theological reflection on modern economic theory. The Radical Orthodox critique should be becoming familiar by now. Long argues that modern capitalist economics is a human construction, not a set of natural, inevitable laws. The belief that a 'free' market is the solution to all questions of human need serves certain power interests. Modern economics tries to divide the world up into 'facts' – which any reasonable person will accept – and 'values', which are only added later and are hard to justify in any scientific way. Values are therefore pushed to the margin, and the market lets rip.

When theology buys into this divided world-view, it makes itself impotent. It can only tag along, allowing secular economists to tell it what the facts of the world are, and offering a superficial religious gloss. It is a short step from this to the secular assumption that religion should be a wholly private affair, an emotional security blanket with nothing to say about how things are or should be.

For Long, however, there are no such things as facts without values. All judgements of factual truth rest upon a value-system. Modern economics takes for granted a view of human nature and worth which puts absolute freedom at the top of the value scale. The problem is that this ideal of freedom doesn't have any content. Freedom itself becomes the good. But freedom without restraint is little more than an exercise of power. Liberal Christians who try to do theology in dialogue with this sort of economics become its lackeys. They end up as cheerleaders for 'a pure formality of freedom that cannot embody the specific content of the Christian tradition, but can see that content only as something to be overcome in order to be relevant to global capitalism' (*DE*, p. 68).

Liberal Christianity, so the argument goes, is embarrassed by the particular claims Christianity traditionally makes, about the call of Israel, the incarnation of God in Jesus Christ, the necessary role of the Church in the plan of salvation, and so on. Set against the 'universal' vision of modernity, these claims look parochial and outdated. However, once we look at where modern secular ideas have come from, we find that they are just as partial, limited, dependent on a particular context. But they refuse to acknowledge the fact. They take refuge in grand but empty ideals of freedom which hide the arbitrary violence and greed of the modern world. Theologians who subordinate Christian claims to these ideals find no way to resist the real murderous injustice of capitalism: 'The problem with this theological economics is that it is so *easily* used, so *readily* relevant. It will not create martyrs' (*DE*, p. 78).

A key element of Long's rejection of modern economics and its theological servants is that it refuses to acknowledge the role played by tradition in forming our ideas of truth and value. As he puts it, 'all rational authority is inseparable from tradition' (*DE*, p. 70). All that we are, think and do happens in a context, a context that is shaped by what we receive from the past, by the communities which pass on memory, wisdom and hope. This is where the contradiction between Christianity and modern economics comes out most starkly:

> An autonomous human freedom cannot provide the basis for tradition because tradition is an inheritance and gift. As gift it always includes more than can be selected: abundance is present. Because Christian theology assumes that the gift arises from God made flesh, the gift is inexhaustible. (*DE*, p. 83)

Modern economic theory assumes that we live in a situation of scarcity. There are only a limited number of goods to go round, so we have to compete and fight for them. Christian theology offers a totally different vision. The true good is given by God, and is always abundant. There is always more than enough. So our life is not defined by competition, but by grace.

Long concedes that liberation theology does try to correct the errors of liberalism. However, it remains trapped by the abstract, modern ideal of justice. For Bell and Long, talk of what is just

18

and good only makes sense in relation to a specific community's story about where it has come from and where it is going. The Christian story, told and performed by the Church, can't be left aside. Values which try to be universal just end up being content-free. There is a 'troubling family resemblance' between liberation theology's idea of justice and the same idea as used by savage capitalism, where it is a mask for violent retribution (*LTEH*, p. 129). To make a break with this cycle of resentment, Christians need to talk about and practise forgiveness and grace.

Long similarly criticizes Rosemary Radford Ruether. Ruether is a feminist liberation theologian. She has sought to recognize and find a way beyond the patriarchy, anti-Semitism and destruction of nature condoned or promoted in parts of the Christian tradition. However, Long argues, this means that she assumes that she can stand outside of tradition, sifting it for what is useful to her ends, and rejecting the bits that don't fit. Her criterion for this is not specifically Christian. It is that familiar modern idea of freedom – a freedom which is detached from history, community and obedience to revelation. In the end, Long claims, Ruether tries to 'pick and choose concepts from the tradition based on the criterion of usefulness' (i.e. what she can use in the cause of freedom). The result is that 'tradition functions as an inert storehouse of ideas activated through human will' (*DE*, p. 118).

We will give Ruether a chance to respond later in the book. For now, just notice the kind of argument being put forward by Radical Orthodoxy. A modern theology – liberal, liberationist, feminist – is analysed down to its core value: freedom. However, because these theologies are critical of Christian tradition, or try to team up with non-Christian allies, they are immediately suspected of heresy. The problem is that they do not stand within the Christian tradition, story and community. They live in no-man's land, pulling their values from the pockets of the capitalists, consumers and politicians who jostle round them. Their much-vaunted 'freedom' is empty, waiting to be filled by anti-Christian ideas of competitive, violent power. We can already see the beginnings of an alternative being proposed: a renewed attention to tradition, a new rootedness in the Church.

A final brief example confirms this Radical Orthodox technique for exposing the fake cures offered by other contemporary theologies. Eco-theology tries to turn around commonly accepted ideas that human beings should lord it over the natural world. It challenges the dualism that gives humanity a godlike spiritual power to dominate the rest of creation, a dualism that has had disastrous effects on our ecosystem. In the process, it criticizes ideas of God as utterly distinct from creation, transcendent, lofty and overpowering. For example, Sallie McFague uses the image of creation as God's 'body' to imply a more intimate, compassionate and worldly relationship between God and nature.

Milbank is scathing about this 'ecological new-ageism' (*WMS*, p. 261). It tries to save nature by turning it into a sacred object or force. However, this forgets that all our ideas of nature are cultural – formed by human beings in definite historical contexts. Nature is not a neutral, safe harbour for values and the divine presence. As Milbank puts it,

> by turning to nature, we cannot really find the key to 'value'. Its beauties we always 'complete', and so produce in language, symbol and artifact as much as discover. And alongside beauty, we encounter also in nature the ambiguous terror of sublimity: overwhelming, unpredictable power, continuous destruction.
>
> (*WMS*, pp. 260–1)

In other words, there is no such thing as pure nature. Nature is always interpreted and shaped by us, by our words, symbols and actions. Nature only makes sense within human community. When eco-theology denies this for the sake of honouring nature, it risks putting an inhuman, destructive power on the throne of God. It takes for granted our modern alienation from nature, and tries to cure this by turning God into a force within nature. This leads to fatalism, a worship of the forces of nature. Denying God's transcendence of creation means that God is no longer free and loving in relation to nature, but is trapped by it. Appeals to nature 'often mask the ruses of human power and ambition', such that the greenest, cuddliest, most eco-friendly Christianity might be at risk of becoming a 'crypto-fascism' (*WMS*, p. 262). It's no wonder that Radical Orthodoxy manages to upset people!

What is important to see, however, is the pattern that is emerging. According to Radical Orthodoxy, a movement which aims to save the world ends up by making the world dead and brutish. Liberal, liberation and eco- theologies are all tarred with the same brush. They are all found wanting, because they assume that there is a way of discovering what the world is like which is independent of tradition (through reason, social science or nature). They put abstract freedom at the top of their value scale. And they often buy into the modern assumption that all the Christian tradition's talk of God's otherness must be bad.

These theologies of freedom are accused of failing to read the tradition properly. They assume that before the enlightened modern world of today, Christians believed in a caricatured, Aunt Sally God – a horrible cosmic dictator, or distant Father. The modern age demands that we set this image aside. The alternative proposed, however, is no better: running after an empty freedom which cannot resist the worst excesses of capitalism; submitting to the impersonal, violent forces which social science says define reality; or worshipping a nature-God, which is the same as worshipping destructive, blind Fate.

Radical Orthodoxy is biting in its criticisms. Whether those criticisms are fair is something to which we will return. At this point, however, we need to explore in more detail what medicine this new theology is offering.

The cure of souls

We've seen that, for Radical Orthodoxy, secularism is a religious myth that pretends to be science. It claims to begin with objective, universal truths – things that no sane or reasonable person could reject. It is therefore guilty – despite its rejection of the supernatural – of not taking the changing, particular, material character of our historical existence seriously.

It is extremely important to underline this point. Despite what its detractors might suspect, Radical Orthodoxy does not assert a religious truth that simply falls out of the heavens. In the introduction to the *Radical Orthodoxy* collection, it is stated that 'for radical orthodoxy, all real knowledge involves some revelation of the infinite in the finite' (*RONT*, p. 5). Radical Orthodoxy tries to take seriously the changing, historical, limited nature of our world, and the cultural context in which all our talk of God takes place. This is not a theology which seeks to abandon reason, or claim some completely otherworldly standpoint from which it dispenses the truth about things. Things are a little more complicated than that – something which Radical Orthodoxy's critics have not always appreciated.

Consider this statement, also taken from *Radical Orthodoxy*:

> The central theological framework of radical orthodoxy is 'participation' as developed by Plato and reworked by Christianity, because any alternative configuration perforce reserves a territory independent of God. The latter can lead only to nihilism (though in different guises). Participation, however, refuses any reserve of created territory, while allowing finite things their own integrity. (*RONT*, p. 3)

Participation is a key category for this theology. It suggests that the world only has being because it shares in the being of God. However, this sharing of being has to be understood in a specific way. Perhaps it is helpful to think of there being two rules which govern Radical Orthodoxy's use of this idea:

- *Rule One* Participation is not identity. The being of the world (or our own human being) is not the same as God's. Only by keeping to this rule do we stop ourselves taking a part of the world and turning it into an object of unlimited worship. This is our protection against idolatry, and all the domination and cruelty which flow from it.
- *Rule Two* Participation does assume a genuine relationship. We can only understand the being of the world in relation to God. It is God's creative act which gives being to the world. It is the same creative act which makes it possible for us to become like

God. The infinite is revealed in and through the finite, limited, worldly, time-bound, material world.

The notion of participation takes the idea of analogy a step further. As we saw previously, recovering an analogical relationship between God and the world is seen as crucial to resisting the new secular religion of power. But, for Radical Orthodoxy, analogy is something dynamic, not just a dry theory about how words work. It is a living way of relating to God, best expressed in Christian life and worship. Analogy leads us to participation in the life of God.

So it is not enough for a theologian merely to accept the idea of analogy. She must also allow her very patterns of thought and existence, her being, to be caught up, lit up and perfected in the being of God. As we have seen, for Radical Orthodoxy, all knowledge involves a revelation of the infinite in the finite. There must be a genuine encounter with God, in which God is not simply an external will or commanding voice, but a surrounding, life-giving, guiding reality.

This accounts for Radical Orthodoxy's view of reason. Reason is not rejected in favour of another source of truth based wholly on authority. That might seem to be the case when we read Milbank saying that 'If my Christian perspective is persuasive, then this should be a persuasion intrinsic to the Christian *logos* itself, not the apologetic mediation of a universal human reason' (*TST*, p. 1), or 'Reason's domain is nihilism; whereas the discovery of a meaningful world governed by a *logos* can only be made by faith' (*BR*, p. 120). However, in both cases, Milbank refers to an alternative 'logos'. 'Logos' is a term which can mean 'word', but generally has a wider meaning: something like 'rational speech' or 'meaningful order'. There is a reason in Christian theology, but it is not the same as the fake reason offered by the secular Enlightenment, which is western prejudice in fancy dress. And so, earlier on the same page as our last quotation from Milbank, we read that 'we must pass beyond the still all-too-modern fideism of neo-orthodoxy, towards a "radical orthodoxy" that refuses the duality of reason over against faith'. Fideism means a position in Christian theology which asserts the claims of faith in the teeth of all rational objection. Milbank is arguing instead that faith and reason can be brought into harmony within a Christian vision. What tends to upset people is his claim that it is *only* within Christian theology that reason is truly reasonable!

In discussing Aquinas and the twentieth-century Catholic theologian Henri de Lubac, Milbank states that 'faith and reason are not essentially distinct, since both are but differing degrees of participation in the mind of God' (*ROCE*, p. 35). It is only by sharing in the light-giving wisdom of God that we can think properly at all.

Why is this? Because any object of thought, and even our own minds, can only be understood if we see them in relation to what has given them being, keeps them in being, and brings them to their perfect end. We come back again to Radical Orthodoxy's claim that, far from leading us away from the world, from time and matter, theology gives the world its true substance and meaning. Time is not strung out over some empty abyss. Matter is not a collection of brute lumpy facts floating in the void. Both matter and time are made up by relationships, and rooted in an original relationship with God. They are gifts of grace, and therefore they can be bearers of meaning: 'for theology there are no "givens" only "gifts" ' (*BR*, p. xi).

In the introduction to *Radical Orthodoxy*, this is the point of the curious phrase 'suspending the material'. The belief that all matter, bodies, culture and time have an eternal source does not lead to an otherworldly spirituality. In fact, it is the only way of ensuring that these realities are given genuine worth. When we experience our bodies as gifts, for example, and not as machines or brute things, we learn to celebrate and delight in them. Modernity reduces everything to one level, draining the world of real worth. Radical Orthodoxy calls on a transcendent reality, which interrupts or 'suspends' worldly reality, giving it back to us as a gift (*RONT*, p. 3). We value the world by seeing it related to God as its giver. Without that relationship, the world is just so much stuff, to be pushed around and exploited as we see fit.

Christianity answers secularism back with its own story of how things are. For Radical Orthodoxy, Christian theology leaves no part of the world empty of God. Reason can only be reasonable if it is lit up by faith. Cut off from God, the world becomes meaningless, a playground for destructive, empty ideologies.

This theological vision therefore has social implications as well. Graham Ward argues that a strong doctrine of participation is necessary to counter the social fragmentation associated with postmodernity, particularly with the effects of cyberspace and globalization (*CG*, p. 75). Christianity can promote the links between our different bodies – physical, social, political, ecclesial – seeing them as interconnected rather than separate and self-contained. We are creatures of desire, and this desire has been hijacked by the marketplace, making us yearn for commodities which can never satisfy our longing for connection.

We will return to Ward's account of desire in Chapter 3. For now, we can just get a hint of his theological vision through the following passage:

> Traditional accounts of the *imitatio Christi* [the imitation of Christ], and doctrines of creation and eschatology, teach that the purpose of human beings is to be sanctified, and the function of the Church, as those who are in the process of sanctification, is to draw all creation back into participation in God – to co-operate with God in the redemption of the world. Christian desire moves beyond the fulfilment of its own needs; Christian desire is always excessive, generous beyond what is asked. (*CG*, p. 75)

Ward summarizes here many of the constructive theological positions advanced by Radical Orthodoxy on the basis of its commitment to participation. It is worth drawing these out in a little more detail.

Creation

Notice how God's purpose in creation, the role of Christ in the life of the believer, and the Christian hope for the fulfilment of God's promises are all held together. This is not a new position in Christian theology, but its significance is only truly brought out when we look in more detail at Radical Orthodoxy's context and controversies.

The role of the doctrine of creation is especially important. Ward notes how much modern economics is based on the doctrine of scarcity. It is a point we have already come across in discussing the work of Stephen Long. The problem with this view is that it assumes that we must always be locked in deadly competition with one another for the resources we need to live. It makes conflict and violence the default reality for human life. Any account of peace and goodness has to be reactive, a secondary attempt to bring order to chaos. However, the attempt will always be futile, like Canute trying to order the incoming tide to retreat. The impersonal forces of scarcity and competition mock our petty efforts to create havens of peace.

This is why Milbank is so critical of much moral philosophy in his caustic essay 'Can Morality be Christian?' The answer he gives to his own question is 'no'. Morality, as we commonly understand it, is reactive. It assumes there is death, suffering and evil out there, and the role of morality is to try to hold back the tide of these bad things. Christianity, according to Milbank, has a fundamentally different view. The doctrine of creation says that God makes the world out of nothing, simply as a free expression of love. There is no pre-existing force, chaos or evil which God has to fight with to bring the world into being. The creation is perfect, peaceful and sufficient for all life. It is not characterized by scarcity but by fullness.

Secular morality is a parasite. It feeds off death and scarcity, and it demands endless sacrifice. It sets up universal laws to try to regulate these threats. In contrast, Christian virtue begins with the belief that 'In the beginning there was only gift: no demon of chaos to be defeated, but a divine creative act; this virtue of giving was not required, was not necessary, and so was a more absolute good, complicit with no threat' (*WMS*, p. 228).

The most arresting part of this claim is that death itself is not part of creation. Sin 'invents' death just as it invents the contrast between good and evil. In the beginning there is only the good, only life. Milbank goes as far as to say:

> It is, of course, quite simply impossible to be a Christian and to suppose that death and suffering belong to God's original plan, or that the struggle of natural selection (which one doubts is even proven as a full account of evolution) is how creation *as creation* rather than thwarted creation genuinely comes about. To do so is to embrace a sickly masochistic faith, against the explicit words of scripture (and one notes here the co-belonging of kenotic and evolutionary Christologies). (*WMS*, p. 229)

Note the sideswipe delivered to Christian theologies which, from Milbank's point of view, have succumbed to the pagan vision of secularism. Kenotic theologies (from the Greek *kenosis* meaning 'emptying') try to make sense of the incarnation of God in Christ by claiming that Christ's divine nature must have been emptied of some of its divine attributes (like omniscience and omnipotence). They attempt to do justice to Jesus' humanity and limitations. Evolutionary theologies go further, questioning the whole idea of God's omnipotence and omniscience, and arguing that God evolves, suffers and celebrates in partnership with the created world. For Milbank, these well-meaning theologies raise a white flag to the secular belief that death is inevitable. They deny God's transcendence, and the gift of God in creation. They are therefore incapable of redeeming us. A full-blooded Christian vision does not shirk from saying that even death was not part of the original creation.

This accords with what Milbank calls the 'ontological priority of peace over conflict' (*TST*, p. 390). This means that peace and harmony are not things we have to cobble together out of the wreckage of the world, but the gifts that come first of all, the gifts that define reality, because they reflect the nature of the giver. God, the Trinity, is peace, is harmony between Father, Son and Spirit. It is an idea Milbank derives from Augustine, who contrasts the heavenly city of peace with the earthly city founded on war. The peace of Rome, Augustine argues, is only a temporary one, based on conquest and death. The peace of God is 'coterminous with all Being whatsoever' (*TST*, p. 392). It has no outside, and therefore no territory which to defend. Only Christian peace is non-violent.

There are critical questions which need to be raised about this account, not least the exact status of Milbank's claim that death is not part of creation. What is important for now is to see how this way of expressing the original peace of creation shapes the Radical Orthodox understanding of Christ and the goal of Christian hope.

The imitation of Christ

If creation is perfect, if evil has no ultimate reality, what is the purpose of God becoming flesh in Christ? Could God not simply correct our illusions by teaching and law? The answer given by John Milbank is complicated, but it can be broken down into several stages.

First, there is no philosophical or historical way of proving that the incarnation is necessary or true. That would be to fall back into the secular assumption that there is some universal set of rules which defines what can be real without reference to God.

Second, this means that our starting point has to be Christian practice, the way in which Christians live by seeking to be shaped by Christ. This might seem contradictory. After all, why would Christians follow Christ if they did not first believe him to be the Son of God? But Milbank is saying that it is only through the actual historical exercise of being affected by and drawn to Christ that ideas of incarnation come about. The practice of the faithful, of the Church, comes first.

In other words, what is primary is a way of life, a pattern of behaviour. Therefore, 'Jesus is significant as the way, the kingdom' and arguments for Jesus' divinity are justified because 'the exemplary narratives of Jesus show us the "shape", and the concrete possibility of a non-violent practice'. This is 'an exemplary practice which we can imitate and which can form the context for our lives together, so that we can call ourselves "the body of

Christ"' (*TST*, p. 396).[3] Christ offers us a story which shows us what it means to live non-violently. By imitating Christ, Christians learn to be shaped by the peaceful will of God, and they become a different sort of community from those founded on competition and conquest.

But does this really do justice to the importance of Christ in Christian tradition? After all, isn't Christ supposed to achieve something for the world, to make atonement for sin and offer grace – not just be an 'example' for us to follow?

Third, therefore, Milbank tries an account of the atonement, of the difference Christ makes to our standing with God. He argues that Jesus' story – particularly the cross – shows us the nature of sin and the essence of goodness. It shows us that sin is 'arbitrary violence' and that goodness is 'infinite generosity' (*TST*, p. 397). On the cross, Jesus reveals what sin is and how it can be overcome, not by reactive moral laws, but by a practice of mutual forgiveness.

Milbank is wary of saying that Christ is a sacrifice for sin, as if sin wields some power or exacts a price which God is forced to pay. Christ 'was an effective sacrifice because he overcame sacrifice once and for all' (*BR*, p. 100). Christ's non-violent death shows that God does not need to fight force with force. God simply goes on giving, as he did in creation.

One of the most striking things Milbank argues is that God does not, strictly speaking, forgive us. God does not need to. As Julian of Norwich pointed out, 'God does not forgive, since he cannot be offended, but only continues to give, despite our rejection of his gift' (*BR*, p. 60). What we call forgiveness, then, is nothing other than the renewal of God's original gift of creation. What needs to happen is that God's gift is mediated to us, and that we learn to forgive one another: 'divine redemption is not God's forgiving us, but rather his giving us the gift of the capacity for forgiveness' (*BR*, p. 162). Christ makes this possible. As human and divine, he is able to offer God's gift to us and our response to God. As the crucified victim, he is able to overcome violence by non-violence. He shows the way – he *is* the way – to the fulfilment of what we are created to be.

Eschatology, sanctification and the Church

Remember that at the heart of Radical Orthodoxy's vision is participation. All creation shares in the nature of God. Human beings are called to do this in a conscious way: 'the natural human destiny that looks towards the supernatural vision of God is only the outworking in a conscious, knowing and willing created nature of the paradox of creation as such: it is of itself nothing, and only exists by participation' (*BR*, p. 114). We participate in God through the forgiveness and generosity that are the essence of peace and harmony.

Radical Orthodoxy shares with Eastern Orthodoxy a strong sense that our destiny is 'deification' – to be made like God. It also speaks of the 'beatific vision' which Aquinas said we were destined to enjoy in heaven. But Radical Orthodoxy interprets this as more than simply looking on the divine perfection. In the beatific vision, we become part of God's divine life.

Radical Orthodoxy's view of humanity is inseparable from this end point. However, as we have already seen, this final beatitude is not individualistic. Ward identifies atomism as one of the defining sins of our age. Radical Orthodoxy, by contrast, aims to be social through and through. Both Milbank and Ward use the image of the city as a sign that human reality is always political and communal. Without this dimension, Christianity becomes a pale reflection of selfish liberalism.

Milbank claims that the practice of forgiveness founds the community of the Church as an alternative political structure, an alternative 'city'. In fact, as we shall see, he gives this a strong twist. The Church is necessary if the atoning work of Christ is to be made available to people, because atonement is nothing more than the creation of a forgiving community: 'Jesus' practice is only atoning in the form of a new social mechanism in which we can be situated' (*TST*, p. 397). Without the Church, Jesus is isolated. He might be a merely historical individual, a good man or teacher. He might be a purely divine saviour, stepping down to earth to rescue souls and take them away to heaven. In either case, the link between God and creation is broken.

Only if Jesus is the first of many brothers and sisters does forgiveness become a reality that changes the world, rather than an external teaching or private spiritual experience. Only as the heart of a community can it 'draw all creation back into participation in God', as Ward puts it. The Church is not an optional extra, but the means by which the reconciliation of God and humanity is realized.

On the one hand, Radical Orthodoxy's vision is universal: all creation exists to participate in God. On the other, it is highly specific. It is the particular story of Jesus which shows us what it means for God and humanity to be reconciled. It is the Church which makes this story a living reality through the way it worships and lives together. Milbank is clear that no 'universal reason' can justify these claims. Only the inner attractiveness of the stories and practices and speculations which are offered can draw people to them.

This makes sense according to the logic of this theology. All creation exists by participation. There is nothing that exists which is not a gift from God. So there cannot be any more all-encompassing reality, or surer ground on which to stand than a theology based on faith in this vision. As we have seen, Milbank argues that part of the reason for believing in the incarnation is that it strengthens the existing Christian practice of forgiveness. The only other reason he offers is 'the inherent attractiveness of the picture of God thence provided: no other picture, save of incarnation in a joyful and suffering life, gives quite such an acute notion of divine love, and involvement in our destiny' (*TST*, p. 384).

Does Radical Orthodoxy do justice to Christian claims about the incarnation? Does it give too great a role to the Church? Is it too exclusive and damning in the way it criticizes other points of view, secular and theological? Is its appeal to 'attractiveness' evidence that it puts greater store by aesthetics than truth? These are some of the questions that we will take into the rest of this book. Before that, however, we will conclude with a brief consideration of Radical Orthodoxy's own story and influences.

Second opinions

Given that Radical Orthodoxy is scathing about the modern world's abandonment of tradition, it is no surprise that much of its work is carried out through a demanding engagement with thinkers and texts from the past. Our discussion so far has already touched on many of these: Plato, Augustine, Aquinas and (negatively) Duns Scotus.

We need to point out that the interpretations given of these thinkers have been strongly challenged. Even some sympathetic to Radical Orthodoxy, such as James Smith, are not convinced that Plato can be given such a prominent role in Christian theology. They worry that his philosophy is too world-denying, too hostile to time and the body (*RORT*, pp. 61–72).

Aquinas has been another hotly disputed figure. For example, John Milbank and Catherine Pickstock claim that Aquinas teaches the doctrine of participation, that our minds share in the divine nature when they are illuminated by truth. This view has been rejected by John Marenbom. He argues that Aquinas claims only that our intellects are derived from God's, not that they share in God's nature (*DRO*, pp. 49–64). Radical Orthodoxy imposes the idea of participation on the texts for its own purposes (prime among which is to deny any role for philosophy independent of theology). This has been a charge raised against its readings of a number of major figures and schools of theology and philosophy. The grand nature of Radical Orthodoxy's vision, it is said, has led it to play fast and loose with careful readings of its forebears.

Aside from such detailed issues of interpretation, it is important to note that Radical Orthodoxy's readings of the tradition happen in a contemporary context. Certain questions and approaches are privileged over others. Before we look in more depth at this new theology's claims, it is worth briefly placing it in its setting.

Radical Orthodoxy has not been alone in questioning some of the assumptions of modern secular liberalism. Milbank points to a 'counter-Enlightenment' tradition, in which thinkers such as Jacobi, Hamann and Kierkegaard called into question the modern faith in pure reason. In the twentieth century, the Reformed theologian Karl Barth attacked the liberal accommodation to the political status quo which in Germany led to unthinking support for the First World War, and devastating compromises with Nazism. He called theology back to its specifically Christian roots in the free self-revelation of God in Christ.

More significant for Radical Orthodoxy was the growth of the so-called *nouvelle théologie* (new theology) in Roman Catholic circles, particularly associated with Yves Congar and Henri de Lubac. On one level, these theologians called the Church back to the writings of the early fathers of the Church as a means of renewing its vision. More specifically, Milbank argues that de Lubac's theology was well on the way to rejecting any 'natural' knowledge of God or pure reason separate from our participation in God: 'there *is* no spiritual, intelligent being (angelic or human) that is not ordered by grace to the beatific vision: that is to deification.'[4] The natural only has being because it is lifted up, oriented to and sharing in the supernatural. This is in contrast to other strands of Catholic reforming thought, which according to Milbank, naturalize the supernatural, reducing the transcendent to a dimension of our own human being.

This might seem like a pedantic point, but it is crucial for Radical Orthodoxy, and explains much of its unease with the reforms of the Second Vatican Council, which signalled a new openness of the Roman Catholic Church to modernity and to liberal ideas such as human rights. In this context, Pickstock's choice of the pre-Vatican II Latin Mass as the supreme liturgy is not accidental. Tracey Rowland also takes Vatican II to task for its uncritical acceptance of the presence of God within secular mass culture. She argues that the Council's affirmation of modern culture was detached from any serious theological framework. In effect, by ignoring the fact that secularism was an anti-Christian ideology, it let it win.[5]

One of the authors to whom Rowland makes extensive reference is Alasdair MacIntyre. And this points us to another important part of Radical Orthodoxy's context. MacIntyre is a key figure in a general 'postliberal' trend in philosophy and theology.

He has argued that rationality and ethics need to be shaped by narratives, by traditions of enquiry and virtue. Modern liberal ethics tries to stand alone, cut off from all such traditions. The result is a morality which is arbitrary, shallow, crisis-driven, individualistic and ultimately incapable of directing the forces unleashed by modern technology. MacIntyre's promotion of 'virtue ethics' has been widely influential. Virtues are what shape a person's character. They are deep-rooted dispositions, formed by the stories and the communities within which a person makes sense of the world.[6]

Postliberal theology has eagerly taken up this baton, and MacIntyre himself has been drawn back to Augustine and Christianity. One of the most important theologians working out the implications of these ideas is Stanley Hauerwas.[7] Many others have followed in this direction. While they may not agree on all points, a family resemblance among them can be made out. They all emphasize the virtue-centred character of Christian ethics. They all argue that these virtues need to be related to fundamental stories, and that these stories need to be told and celebrated and lived out by communities. Liturgy and the Church thus become absolutely vital in forming Christians. And always, this formation happens against a backdrop of antagonism to modern secular liberalism, which is condemned for its rootless superficiality, and for being little more than a disguise for the violence of capitalism.

An important voice in postliberal theology has been George Lindbeck. His seminal work, *The Nature of Doctrine*, draws a sharp contrast between interpretations of how doctrine (teaching) is understood in the Church.[8] The 'experiential-expressive' model assumes that there is a common human core of religious experience which is dressed up (expressed) in different languages. Behind the Church's language, therefore, there is something ineffable but universal. This is essentially the standpoint of liberal theology. Against this, Lindbeck puts forward the 'cultural-linguistic' model. This claims that the specific language of the Church is more than window-dressing. In fact, people and their world are shaped by language. And the language we speak is embedded in our culture and community. This means that we can't get rid of the Church and its creeds and teachings to get at some universal essence of religion. That essence is a myth of liberal modernity, a nothing, a blank. No: language, culture and community are what come first. They shape the kind of experience we have of the world (indeed they shape the kind of world we experience at all).

Of course, there is far more to the work of MacIntyre, Hauerwas, Lindbeck and their sympathizers than these very brief comments can tell. There are also points on which they and Radical Orthodox writers disagree (Milbank typically does not think that MacIntyre and Lindbeck go far enough). What is important to note, however, is that Radical Orthodoxy has not happened in a vacuum. It is part of a wider trend in theology which is extremely critical of liberalism and secularism, and which seeks to use the resources of tradition and liturgy to renew the Church's role in defining what is true and good and beautiful.

The publication of *Post-Secular Philosophy* in 1998 also marked a watershed. Increasingly, theologians were engaging with cutting-edge continental philosophical thinkers, and finding that there were opportunities to express religious and theological standpoints once more. Postmodern thought was ready to move beyond the secularism of liberal modernity, to re-enchant the world.

Radical Orthodoxy's own story is one of growing influence, controversy and dialogue. John Milbank's work undoubtedly gave the movement its major impetus through the early 1990s, culminating in the publication of the *Radical Orthodoxy* collection and subsequent series of books. Its origins are very specific. Along with Milbank, the other pioneers of the movement, Catherine Pickstock and Graham Ward, were both based in Cambridge University in the United Kingdom. All three were Anglicans of a particular Anglo-Catholic style, in which the liturgy of the Eucharist is central.

The title of the movement reflects these origins. It is 'orthodox' because it takes the traditional Christian dogmas and creeds of the early, patristic period as normative. That orthodoxy is supposed to transcend the denominational divisions of Christianity, and avoid the errors of both liberal and conservative theologies of the modern era. It is 'radical' because it appeals to the roots of the Christian tradition and uses that tradition to go on a militant offensive against secularism. But it is also radical because it uses postmodern philosophy to restate Christian tradition, and restore depth and worth to material, embodied life (*RONT*, pp. 2–3). Radical Orthodoxy seeks to be ecumenical in its scope, appealing to a range of Christian traditions beyond its Anglican beginnings. It also tries to hold together postmodernism and Christian tradition without being nostalgic for past glories, or simply swimming with current cultural trends. Whether it succeeds will be one of the questions running through this book.

Since the days of its birth and consolidation, however, the movement has diversified, and, arguably, begun to show divisions. *Radical Orthodoxy* included Roman Catholic authors, one of whom – Laurence Hemming – went on to edit *Radical Orthodoxy? A Catholic Enquiry*. In this volume, he raised some criticisms of Radical Orthodoxy's view of the Church, which he claimed needed to be founded on something solid (like the authority of the Pope). From a contrary point of view, contributors to *Radical Orthodoxy and the Reformed Tradition* have voiced concerns. They worry that the emphasis on our 'participation' in God blurs the otherness of God, and refuses to affirm the freedom and integrity of creation. And, as we have mentioned, one of the authors in the 'Radical Orthodoxy' series, James K. A. Smith, questions the version of Plato put forward by Milbank and Pickstock.

Smith has also taken Graham Ward to task for his refusal, at the end of *Cities of God*, to pass judgement on other faith traditions.[9] Indeed, the direction taken by Ward has often had a distinctive emphasis. He is far more sympathetic to Derrida, for example, a figure heavily lambasted by Milbank and Pickstock for nihilism. Ward is also apparently more open to dialogue with other disciplines, such as cultural theory and queer studies, and so more willing to discuss how the claims of Christian theology are always conditioned by their context.

Some of these issues will be treated at greater length in the rest of this book. It is not always clear whether they represent substantial divisions or merely differences of emphasis. For now it is worth noting that Radical Orthodoxy seems to be at a pivotal moment. Ward and Milbank have long since moved on from their Cambridge positions. Milbank's posting at the University of Virginia (before his return to the UK) helped to ensure a significant North American discussion of the movement. Regular international conferences and publications have continued to sustain it. In the meantime, bibliographical resources and surveys to promote study of the movement have begun to appear.

All of this would appear to bode well for Radical Orthodoxy. However, the weight and urgency that accompanied the first volumes of the 'Radical Orthodoxy' series seems to have dissipated. Differences between key figures in the movement may turn out to be more significant than is currently appreciated. It has also been subjected to increasingly substantial criticism. Does this 'new theology' have a future?

The path ahead

If we are to have any chance of answering this question, we need to look in more depth at what this movement is based on. The chapters to come will look in more detail at some of the big questions which have been at the centre of Radical Orthodoxy's claims and disputes.

We began by asking whether Radical Orthodoxy coops theology up in its own isolated world and language. It has become clear over our discussion so far that it would reject this way of putting the matter. Instead, Milbank and others have argued that it is the secular world which is shut in on itself, dead to God and dominated by a vicious cycle of brutality and bureaucracy.

On the final page of Bret Easton Ellis's novel *American Psycho*, the serial killer whose public face is that of a respectable businessman is confronted with a despairing sign in a bar: 'this is not an exit'. For all the extremity of the violence committed by the killer, he is continually mistaken for other people, his crimes are undetected (perhaps even only imagined), and his peers carry on their obsession with materialism and shallow social esteem. He seems destined to continue the empty, meaningless round of consumerism and sadism for all eternity. This is an extreme depiction of the world out of which Radical Orthodoxy seeks to break us. But to do so, it must take us back to the Christian community of the Church, to its traditions, scriptures and worship. Only there can our eyes and hearts be opened. Only there can we exchange meaningful signs with one another and with God.

A key issue that will guide us will therefore be *communication*. Is Radical Orthodoxy saying that the truth is only for 'insiders' to the Church? Can there be any dialogue between Christians and those with alternative views? More generally, how does the Church speak to those beyond the community of faith? Can Christian theology adopt the language of other disciplines without betraying its distinctiveness? Or is it right in accusing secular society of imposing a flat, uniform, vision of the world that leaves no room for a religious view?

The justification for this is rooted both in the wider philosophical context and in Radical Orthodoxy's own positioning. More broadly, the 'turn to language' has been a major feature of philosophy over the last two hundred years, spilling over into sociology, psychology, cultural and media studies. We are more than ever aware that what and how we communicate is shaped by particular languages and grammars. Meaning is determined by how words are used, and in what contexts. Language is a vital, creative force in its own right. This insight has opened up new possibilities for interpretation, at the same time as heightening our uncertainties about how we connect language with truth and reality.

As we will see, Radical Orthodoxy embraces the turn to language. It argues that language and truth need to be understood in relation to a dynamic view of Christian doctrine. Creation, incarnation, Church and Eucharist become some of the key focal points for establishing how Christianity gives language its power and depth. But they are also important points of distinction between Christianity's story and those of other faiths and ideologies. The restoration of true communication means refusing those approaches which, according to Radical Orthodoxy, lead only to the violent, amoral abandonment of transcendence.

This follows from the movement's choice of participation as a central theme. For humanity and creation to participate in God, genuine communication and communion must be possible. An 'analogical' world-view is commended, in which the mundane world only has being and meaning because it constantly refers us to its divine source. Analogy implies that our words are not stuck like rats in a maze. They mediate another reality to us. And, for Radical Orthodoxy, this makes language potentially sacramental. If it is used in the right context, it does more than describe God. In the Eucharist, for example, it actually makes it possible for us to share in the divine nature.

Communication is therefore a dynamic reality, consisting of words, actions and sacraments. By using it as a way of structuring our exploration of Radical Orthodoxy, we are attempting to catch something of its spirit, at once recovering an ancient analogical approach and yet also assimilating the postmodern fascination with signs.

We can look at communication from different angles. First, we can examine how language itself works. Second, we can explore the nature of community, the social context in which communication happens. Third, we can consider what motivates and directs communication. What is it we want when we try to connect with others, or with a divine Other?

Language, community and desire: these are the central facets of Radical Orthodoxy's vision of theology. These will be the themes which shape the next three chapters of this book. The fourth chapter will review in more detail some of the major criticisms of the movement which have been advanced. Debate and disagreement are also part of the story of how this feisty theological vision has been shaped and communicated.

The concluding chapter will also offer a forward-looking view of where the debate could go from here. It will sketch a Christian theology which learns from Radical Orthodoxy's insights, but recovers a more authentic Christian affirmation of the worldliness of creation, the openness of community and the imperative of dialogue.

That still lies ahead. Now, we turn to the first of our major topics, language. Does Radical Orthodoxy offer a 'Word made strange' – or simply a lot of incomprehensible words?

Chapter summary

Radical Orthodoxy makes a number of bold claims.

- No part of the world can be understood apart from God.
- The idea of an independent secular realm is something we have invented.
- Secular philosophies claim to be based on pure reason. However, they are really Christian theology gone bad, religions of power promoting violence.
- Liberal and other progressive theologies play into the hands of secularism, accepting that the world can be known independent of its relationship to God. Conservative theologies try to reintroduce God into the world from the outside. Both fail to overcome the problems created by the creation of a secular world.
- The cure for this secular disease is a recovery of Christian tradition and community.
- The key elements of Christianity are participation, a dynamic sharing in the nature of God; and the belief that death and violence are secondary to God's gift of peace in creation, renewed in Christ.
- Christian faith saves the world from becoming the plaything of impersonal forces. It treats creation as a gift, not a given.

However, we have also raised some initial questions about its project.

- Is it right to say that all secular thinking is pagan and anti-Christian?
- Does it stop theology and the Church from seeing God at work outside Christianity?
- Does it put barriers in the way of the Church's communication with non-Christians?
- Does it offer an adequate account of Christian doctrines like the incarnation?

1

Language: telling God's story

Near the end of *After Writing*, Catherine Pickstock is discussing the words attributed to Jesus in the gospel accounts of the Last Supper, and spoken again by the priest at the Eucharist as the bread and wine are consecrated. She makes the following claim: 'The words of Consecration "This is my body", therefore, far from being problematic in their meaning, *are the only words which certainly have meaning, and lend this meaning to all other words*' (*AW*, p. 264; emphasis in original).

This seems to be an extraordinary thing to say. The words she quotes have been the subject of intense controversy within the Church since the Reformation. To those outside the Church, they might sound strange, superstitious or simply irrelevant. How on earth, then, can they be put forward as the key to all meaning and the anchor of language?

The crisis of language

Part of the answer to this involves understanding how language has become a core issue and problem for modern thinking. The Danish philosopher Kierkegaard tells a couple of little parables which point in this direction:

> In a theatre, it happened that a fire started offstage. The clown came out to tell the audience. They thought it was a joke and applauded. He told them again, and they became still more hilarious. This is the way, I suppose, that the world will be destroyed – amid the universal hilarity of wits and wags who think it is all a joke.[1]

> What philosophers say about actuality is often just as disappointing as it is when one reads on a sign in a secondhand shop:

Pressing Done Here. If a person were to bring his clothes to be pressed, he would be duped, for the sign is merely for sale.[2]

Written in the first half of the nineteenth century, these tragi-comic little episodes point to what some have called a crisis of representation. European philosophy had become more radical in its doubts, less inclined to base itself upon theology and revealed faith. The scientific method progressed through hypothesis and experimentation. Theories had to be tested, not accepted on authority. And science cast doubt upon the capacity of religious belief to explain the world. These shifts of ideas were accompanied by huge social transformations, which uprooted settled patterns of life through industrial revolution and the growth of large urban centres where the new working and middle classes mingled on public streets.

In Kierkegaard's day, the feudal hierarchies still had power, but it was changing, if not waning in the face of the new capital and its bourgeois masters. And so a wider sense of the cosmos as an ordered whole, with graded levels of being reaching up to God, was trembling. New disciplines of study and investigation challenged the supremacy of theology. Allegory – the mystical connections between different levels of meaning – was giving way to one-level, historical criticism. Mechanistic explanations were supplanting supernatural and purposive ones.

Kierkegaard's parables point out more subtle aspects of this situation. In the first, we see the problem of knowing what is real (and urgent) in a theatrical setting. The new leisured classes had become consumers of entertainment. Increasingly, as Kierkegaard makes clear elsewhere, their consumption was driven by the media, which shaped opinions and tastes. In fact, the media's influence was becoming so strong, that the lines between fiction and reality were being blurred (there is an echo of the contemporary obsession with reality TV). Was something reported because it was real, or did it become real because it was reported?

The second parable also introduces a note of radical uncertainty about signs. The context in which a sign is used can fundamentally change its meaning. And this leads to anxiety. If nothing is fixed, what stable reference points do we have for sorting out truth from lies? In Kierkegaard's story, this fear is given a commercial twist. The sign is for sale. In the burgeoning capitalist economy, was reality anything more than a collection of commodities to be bought and sold? Was meaning anything but market value?

In this setting, hugely influenced by the forces of media and capital, it is understandable that the relationship between knowledge and reality was called into question. Could thoughts mediate higher levels of reality to us? Could they even connect with the everyday reality around us? Or were they only human productions, whose meaning shifted and changed through history and across cultures? Could they only give us access to appearances rather than the things themselves, relative truths rather than absolutes?

The Romantic movement (associated with poets like Wordsworth and Coleridge in England, and writers like Schlegel, Novalis and the young Schleiermacher in mainland Europe) reacted against the mechanism and dry rationalism of some Enlightenment thought. They valued the creative genius and the spontaneity of art, which could tap into deep wells of feeling and give us a spiritual connection with the eternal and infinite. However, Romanticism itself had an ambiguous relationship to traditional Christian belief. It was unclear whether the infinite was another name for God, or for a dimension of human creativity, a spur for poetic production.

All in all, then, the nineteenth century bequeathed a restless uncertainty about the grounds for secure knowledge, and our relationship to objective reality 'out there', beyond our minds and hearts. It is in this context we need to understand the developments which grew out of that time, but which only came to fruition in the twentieth century, and which John Milbank calls 'the linguistic turn'.

The turn to language: stories and performances

Kierkegaard was one of the philosophers who began to call attention to the importance of language in mediating thought and reality to us. Milbank points to other examples of this trend, some reaching back into the eighteenth century (*WMS*, p. 84). An increasing awareness of cultural and historical change was the catalyst for this.

Words came to be seen as not merely containers for timeless truths, or labels which are stuck on to individual things. To have meaning, words must be *used*. And they are used in a context – alongside other words, and in particular times and places. Words do not drop down ready made from heaven. They are not things already out there in the world waiting to be discovered by us. Words are social constructions. Languages are cultural. Two people using different languages will see and experience the world in different ways. Languages, each with their own history, definitions and grammar, shape reality in distinctive ways. The work of learning another tongue, or of translating something into another language, is a work of interpretation. Mechanically trying to substitute one word for another will result in a bad translation, because a language is a structure, with shapes and patterns of its own. It is not a tool kit where each piece works independently of the rest.

One of the most significant philosophers of language in the twentieth century was Ludwig Wittgenstein. In his early work, Wittgenstein had tried to map out what we could say about reality, and he assumed that words were essentially pictures of things. In his later work, however, this approach was fundamentally changed.[3]

Wittgenstein came to see that words were not just signposts, pointing beyond themselves to bits of the world. He could no longer ignore the relationships between words themselves. He compared the way we use language to the rules that govern an activity like a game (hence the term 'language-game', which is often used to summarize Wittgenstein's point).

Imagine a game like football. In order to play the game, we have to know what things are permitted, what the aim of the game is, what counts as a valid score, and so on. In other words, we have to know the rules. Those rules define what football is and how it should be played. They don't simply act as labels for things on the field. The rules provide a framework in which playing the game becomes possible. They decide the validity and meaning of various objects and actions.

Different games have different rules. You can't apply the checkmate rule to badminton, or say that someone is offside in tennis. It just doesn't make sense, not because of the physical attributes of the pitch or equipment, but because the game is what it is only because of the rules. It's not that they describe everything that happens on the field of play. A vast, possibly infinite variety of moves is still possible. But if they go beyond the rules, then they are fouls or out of bounds, or they simply do not make sense. They are not part of the game.

Wittgenstein argued that language works something like this. The meaning it has depends on the context in which it is used, and the way in which it is used. And the contexts are social, cultural ones. The language we use in a legal case will play by different rules to that used in putting on a play, or telling a joke.

The argument can be applied to religion. Religious believers use language in a way determined by the context of their faith. In Christianity, for example, the creeds and scriptures and rituals of the Church provide ways of organizing the way believers speak about God.

It is important to recognize two things in this account of language. First, we should not get too hung up by the word 'games'. Games are chosen as particularly good examples of rule-governed behaviour. There is no suggestion that all language use is playful or frivolous. The principle can be applied to the most deadly serious situations (confessing one's faith, passing sentence, getting married). Second, we should not be too distracted by the legal side of rules, as if using language were about rigidly following a set of commands. For one thing, that does not sound like a good description of what Christians have understood the gospel to be about. The important thing to remember is that 'rules' do shape behaviour and usage, but they are also permissive. They empower and enable us to experience and be certain things. For example, one of the 'rules' of Christian speech might be that we should always speak of life as a free gift of God. This rule sets us free to experience life in a certain way, and does not work like a burdensome 'command'.

George Lindbeck, whose work on doctrine was mentioned in the Introduction, is clearly influenced by Wittgenstein's approach. He argues that culture and language come before experience. They are what shape our access to the world. And he further argues that Christian doctrine works like the grammar of a language, as rules for making Christian life and worship possible.

Several important consequences flow from this approach to language and to Christian language in particular:

- *The importance of community.* Language is not a private activity. It is inherently social. But more than this, to understand any specific language, we have to pay attention to the specific communities in which it is used, and which it helps to shape. In Christian terms, this means that we can't understand Christian language and teaching without taking seriously the Church as the social context in which such language is used.

- *The importance of performance.* The imagery of games is a very practical one. And this connects with the insights of thinkers such as John Austin, a key figure in what has become known as speech-act theory. Briefly, this is the idea that words are not just passive signs. They do things, or rather we do things with words. We can use words to pass judgement, make a promise, seal a business contract, propose and get married. Words are performative. In a Christian context, this means that we have to pay attention to the way Christian life is lived, and what Christians seek to do with words. Within this, a particular focus of attention will be worship, in which words are used to praise, confess, intercede, bless and so on. Sacramental worship – such as Baptism and the Eucharist – takes on special importance. All worship might be said to change the reality of those who take part in it, but the sacraments do so in a particularly direct way. The words and material signs used do not just point beyond themselves to a divine reality, they bring that reality into the world (remembering that this is due to the faithfulness and grace of God, not human power).

- *The need to be an insider.* Games can be spectator sports. But even then, watching is not the same as taking part. And some activities demand that one is a participant in order to fully understand and appreciate them. This is true of religious belief, on this account. Those who do not have faith and are not part of the believing, worshipping community of the Church can only have a meagre grasp of what the faith entails. It is something that must be lived from the inside. Otherwise, one's perception of reality will not be shaped by the language of faith. The temptation to judge the faith by criteria drawn from different language communities is misguided.

- *The threat of relativism.* One of the main concerns raised about this approach is that it seems to isolate different language games from one another. Chess and tennis are entirely separate. The rules of one have no bearing on the rules of the other. But it would be nonsense to say that the rules of chess are 'correct' while those of tennis are not. They are simply different. In a similar way, it could be argued that it is a mistake to say that evolutionary science and Christian belief in creation contradict one another, when in fact we have two different language games, organized to do different things. This has the advantage of getting round tired debates between science and religion. But is it a sleight of hand?

  The worry is that religion and science have nothing to say to one another, and appear to be utterly separate. But how can this square with a Christian belief in the unity of creation, or a scientist's conviction that all truth claims must be backed up by evidence? How does it account for scientists who seek to integrate religious belief and science? More generally, does the attempt to carve up our world into different language games leave us unable to communicate, or offer interpretations and criticisms across the boundaries of those games? Even staying with religion, does it mean that different faith traditions have nothing to say to one another, that they are simply playing by different rules? And should this extend to different traditions within religions (like the various Christian denominations)?

The ghost haunting this particular feast is relativism, the belief that it is simply not possible to compare different belief systems and judge their relative worth. All that can be said is that they work or do not work for those inside them, for those already playing the game. Outsiders have nothing worthwhile to add.

Notice how our view of how language works can have such a powerful effect upon how we understand complex phenomena, human behaviour and even the nature of reality itself. Notice too how the different facets listed above are related. Having a strong view of how a particular community's language shapes the world and needing to be an active performer of that community's stories leads to concerns about relativism and sectarianism.

Lindbeck and others would reject the charge that they are advocating relativism. But they do think that truth is more complicated than simply matching our words to things outside us. They argue that it is a community's whole way of belief and life and worship which can be true to reality. Truth is something performed, lived. And it is, ultimately, people who are true, or who speak truly, not things.

This is a typically 'postliberal' way of approaching the matter. We began by talking about a crisis of representation which afflicted European thought from the eighteenth century onwards. Secular liberalism tried to resolve that crisis by setting up universally binding standards of truth. Reason had to be set free from its cultural limitations and from religious domination.

However, as the last chapter made clear, many now think that liberalism's attempt at coming up with a universal set of rules for thinking and acting was bound to fail. It was deluded, because human beings cannot climb up out of their history, language and culture and take a God's-eye view of everything. When they try, all they succeed in doing is setting up their own limited (European) versions of reason and morality as absolute truths. And this is the ideology that underlies imperialism and racism.

Postliberals want to distance themselves from this project. The turn to language can come to their aid. On the surface, it might look as if making language central to thought would only cut us off more deeply from any transcendent reality. If all we think and know has to come to us via shifting human language, how can we ever encounter the divine? However, postliberals argue that this is only one possible way which the turn to language can go. It can also help to revive religion and liturgy as specific ways to shape the world, which cannot be reduced to science, or any secular set of ideas. In fact, it can help theology go back on the offensive, showing how the secular world's rules are not the only ones.

Before we turn more specifically to Radical Orthodoxy, it is worth introducing another element in this turn to language. Ferdinand de Saussure wrote his *Course in General Linguistics* in 1919. Its influence on subsequent scholarship in this area cannot be over-stated, partly because of the astonishing simplicity of its central argument. Perhaps the best way of explaining Saussure's under-standing of language is that used by Don Cupitt:

> Look up a word in a dictionary. There you find that its origin, its history and its various uses and meanings are all explained in terms of other words. Some of these may be unfamiliar to you, so you go on to look them up as well – and soon you find yourself brows-ing, wandering back and forth through the book indefinitely. One word leads to another, and so on forever . . . You cannot consult this book (or indeed, any other book) unless you already belong within the world of language. The dictionary cannot initiate you into language: it can only refine your grasp of the nuances in a field of differential relationships between words, a field in which you already stand.[4]

Cupitt asks us to notice that the meaning of the printed words is not a hidden 'reality' somewhere apart from the book. The mean-ing of the marks on the page is only ever given as other marks on the page. Saussure made this point by saying that language has no 'positive' terms. By this, he meant that there are no words in language which immediately hook up to reality. Words are always defined by their relationships to and differences from other words.

Saussure of course had much more to say about language and how it signified, but this basic insight was explosive. In European thought, it led in two different directions. Some used this theory of language as a tool to understand how human beings organized reality in significant ways. They were called 'structuralists' because they based their interpretations on what they took to be the underlying patterns or structures of thought – structures which appeared in different cultures across time. The structuralists saw language as a system, and they had something of the Enlightenment ambition to come up with universal rules which would explain human behaviour.

However, not all were convinced by this enterprise. A number of philosophers in the 1960s, including Jacques Derrida, argued that no 'system' or 'structure' of reality could ever be complete. They put together two ideas. First, all language is woven out of differences. Therefore, there is no part of language that we can raise above the rest as the key, or foundation of a system which will explain everything else. There are no master words which decipher the code of language. Second, language exists in time. It takes time even to say or read the simplest statement. And so the meaning of language can never be gathered into a simple, eternal moment of truth.

Difference and time cannot be shaken off. They will ensure that any system or structure, no matter how all-encompassing it sets out to be, will always have a blind spot. It will always leave something out, or be open to an interpretation which it did not predict. Language will always subvert those who try to make absolute truth out of it.

Philosophers like Derrida became known (imaginatively) as post-structuralists. Now that structuralism itself is no longer the talk of dinner parties, terms like 'postmodernist' are more often used. Postmodern is itself a slippery word, which has been used with different meanings in art, architecture, literature and philosophy. What is important from our point of view is that it calls into question the modern, liberal Enlightenment project of setting up universal rules, systems and structures to capture or direct reality. It also calls time on the big stories (the grand narratives) which the modern world used to fill the gap left by the retreat of Christianity: the liberal belief in progress, for example, or the

Marxist idea that the triumph of the proletariat and the establishment of a utopian communist state was an historical inevitability.

Postmodernism has been highly controversial. There have been debates about whether it is truly something new, or just another phase or crisis of modernity. But there have also been sharp accusations that, like postliberalism, it leads to relativism. If meaning never arrives, if truth is simply a matter of difference and definition, then how can we talk about meaning and truth at all? Aren't we just left with irony, detachment and a play of signs which signify nothing?

It might be expected that Radical Orthodoxy simply dismisses postmodernism as a symptom of our contemporary sickness. However, things are not so simple. As we have already noted, we find some withering attacks on Derrida and other postmodern thinkers in the work of Milbank, Pickstock and others. But, at least in some respects, they also want to claim the mantle of post-modernism for themselves. Graham Ward, for example, has argued that Derrida's work supports the view that 'language is always and ineradicably theological'.[5]

In his essay 'The Linguistic Turn as a Theological Turn', Milbank makes the case that Christianity alone truly anticipates the idea that reality is shaped by language through and through. As he puts it 'the post-modern embracing of a radical linguisticality, far from being a "problem" for traditional Christianity, has always been secretly promoted by it' (*WMS*, p. 85).

What does Milbank mean by this claim? According to his argument, the modern turn to language was in fact brought about by Christian thinkers who were spelling out the implications of distinctively Christian belief. In the time of the early and medieval Church, the full implications of these beliefs had not been realized. Theologians of those eras still thought they needed to believe in the reality of fixed substances – something firm on which language could get a grip. Otherwise, if everything was in flux, then chaos would reign. Nothing would have any essential identity, and truth could not be defined.

However, later Christian thinkers began to suspect that this view of language was not consistent with Christian teaching. Vico argued that the belief that reality is made up of fixed substances was the relic of a pagan world-view. Remember that Radical Orthodoxy, following Augustine, sees paganism as a religion of violence, which only achieves peace by conquest. For paganism, violence and chaos come first, and order has to be forced upon it. The same can be said of ancient pagan views of language. The world was viewed as a chaos. Language imposed order on chaos by identifying things which were centres of power and substance.

Against this, Vico and others proposed a more authentically Christian view of language, which was dynamic, interactive and based on relationships. The doctrine of the Trinity became the key. Christians believe that God is not an isolated, undifferentiated substance, but is made up of relationships between the Persons of the Trinity. Relation and communication come first. Fixed identities are a later construction, a fiction.

We seem to have come up against a paradox. At the start of this chapter, we found Catherine Pickstock making a dramatic claim that the Christian Eucharist provides the key to all meaning. And yet here we see Milbank denying that there are any stable substances. Isn't he leading us back into relativism? If there is no anchor for our language and particularly for our talk about God, can we avoid getting swept away by the secular, pluralistic tide? How can Radical Orthodoxy still claim that Christianity is true?

There is no doubt that Radical Orthodoxy makes some big claims for Christianity. Pickstock is by no means alone. Milbank writes that 'theology itself is a social science and the queen of the sciences' (*TST*, p. 380). He says that '*Only* Christianity, once it has arrived, really appears ethical at all' (*TST*, p. 362).

We have already seen how theology is set up in opposition to modern secularism, which is condemned for its nihilism. But notice how Milbank goes further than this: 'only Christian theology now offers a discourse able to position and overcome nihilism itself. This is why it is so important to reassert theology as a master discourse; theology, alone, remains the discourse of non-mastery' (*TST*, p. 6).

This is where we need to tread carefully. It is easy to read such statements as the ultimate in intellectual arrogance. How can these theologians possibly assert their superiority over all other forms of knowledge? However, when we take a closer look, we find that curious paradox rising to the surface again: theology is a 'master discourse', because it is the only discourse of 'non-mastery'. What is going on here?

The story of everything

So far, we have seen how the 'turn to language' has resulted in a greater awareness of how our thought and experience of the world is shaped by language, and so by our historical and cultural context. We have seen how, for postliberals, this means that being part of a community is necessary for sharing its view of the world. At the same time, postmodern sceptics have been arguing that there can be no overarching, absolute system of knowledge or truth. Language always escapes being gathered and locked in the sheepfold.

In a strange way, these two streams of thought have come together to create a new opportunity for Christian theology to reclaim its place. The argument goes something like this. Secular liberalism wanted to do away with the influence of Christian institutions and traditions on the search for truth and on the political organization of society. It believed that Christianity was too irrational, and too limited. Christians believed in things on the basis of revelation and authority. And the things they believed in were not truths which could ever command universal agreement. The idea that our salvation depended upon God becoming a man at a specific point in history seemed far too parochial. So, secularism needed to find a new foundation for truth, one which was universal, accessible to all and self-evident, needing no religious authority to back it up.

The key figures in the development of this kind of thinking were Descartes and Kant. Descartes remained part of the religious world that was passing away. But he began the project of modern philosophy by setting out to doubt everything that was not self-evident and certain. The result was that he ended up with the one thing that could not be doubted, that he himself existed: 'I think, therefore I am.' Descartes then has the problem of how to build up knowledge of the world outside again. The important thing for our purposes, however, is that he gave thought a new starting point. Human reason now had a sure foundation in its own powers of thought.

Kant took up the challenge of trying to justify the objectivity of our knowledge, that is, that my knowledge of the world was based on sure foundations, and could be shared by all rational people. Kant believed that we did not know reality in itself. We could only know the appearances of things. But these appearances had to be linked together and shaped by ideas like cause and effect, substance and identity, and so on. In a sense, it was our minds that shaped reality in order to know it, rather than reality imposing itself upon our minds. However, because Kant was convinced that the world had to be structured in a certain way to be knowable at all, he believed he had shown that knowledge was objective, secure, rational and universal.

Kant extended this argument to his views on ethics and religion. Ethical values had to be universal. I could only believe something to be a duty for me if I believed it to be a duty for all. And religion had to be kept 'within the limits of reason alone'. The teachings of the Church could not be accepted on authority, but only on the basis of reason. Doctrines about Jesus were secondary to following the ethical teaching of Jesus.

Descartes and Kant still thought it was necessary to believe in the existence of God, but this was a God who played his part in a rational system, as an ideal of reason, or a guarantee that knowledge and values still had a foundation or a goal. But the key Christian doctrines of creation, the incarnation, the centrality of the death and resurrection of Christ, the Trinity, the Church, the sacraments – all of these suddenly looked intellectually unnecessary, if not positively harmful.

Secular liberal philosophy therefore has two faces. One face is sceptical. It doubts everything that is asserted by authority alone. The other face looks for new certainty. To replace religious myth, it advances rational and scientific truth. And to achieve this, it must set up new foundations for thought and for values.

Postliberals, in common with Radical Orthodoxy, challenge this two-faced secular stance. They do not, however, simply argue that we have to turn back the clock, and return to a time when the authority of the Church or the scriptures was dominant. Their argument is more interesting than that. They say that secularism isn't sceptical *enough*. It places far too much faith in the power of unaided human reason to provide a foundation for truth. As we saw in the Introduction, a key part of Radical Orthodoxy's rejection of the secular is that this faith in reason hides the murkier reality of a domineering, violent will to power.

What is the alternative? If there are no foundations for truth, are the sceptics right? Are we just left with relativism?

One of the striking things about Radical Orthodoxy is just how far it goes in accepting this conclusion. On the first page of *Theology and Social Theory*, we read that neither secularism nor Christian orthodoxy are rationally justifiable, and that 'The book can, therefore, be read as an exercise in sceptical relativism' (*TST*, p. 1). There simply are no universally recognized foundations for truth.

Once we accept this, however, we start to understand that the way is opened for particular world-views to tell their story of reality without embarrassment. If secularism is just one more story, it can't have the last word. So the Christian story can once more be told and heard. Postmodern scepticism clears away the prejudices of the Enlightenment against anything which is not a self-evident, almost mathematical truth.

Milbank therefore goes on to say that 'If my Christian perspective is persuasive, then this should be a persuasion intrinsic to the Christian *logos* itself, not the apologetic mediation of a universal human reason' (*TST*, p. 1). In other words, the Christian story has to simply recommend itself *as a story*. There's no way of rationally proving it to be true by some criteria alien to it. It has to be an attractive, compelling way of understanding the world. Pascal once said famously that 'the heart has its reasons of which the reason knows nothing'. Something similar might be said about this version of Christianity: it has its own reasons, of which secular rationality is unaware. And that's no bad thing, because secularism is not really rational at all. It is a religion of power.

Radical Orthodoxy wants to put forward a Christian vision that is cheerfully aware that it is no more than a story – and yet at the same time it claims that this story is the one that encompasses all others. It is, as Milbank says, a 'metadiscourse', a story which stands over and above all others. But hasn't postmodernism shown that all stories which try to be that big are destined to collapse under the weight of their own pretensions? Who on earth can tell a story that takes in everything?

It is worth pausing at this point to look in a little more detail at this other key element of the postliberal view of language: the importance of story or narrative.

Narrative theology has been around for some decades. It is closely related to postliberalism, because it rejects the idea that one can do away with the myths and stories of religion in order to find a universal truth behind them. Stories are not just decoration. They are necessary, because we give meaning to our life by telling stories about it. In stories, we can do justice to the nature of human life, to time, relationships and to the growth of character and virtues.

The impact of narrative theology upon Radical Orthodoxy can be seen in phrases like this one from Milbank: 'narrative is our primary mode of inhabiting the world and it characterizes the way the world happens to us, not primarily, the cultural world which humans make' (*TST*, p. 359). Reality comes to us via stories: 'Objects and subjects are, as they are narrated in a story.'[6] Milbank also writes of a 'narrative knowledge' in distinction from 'modernist secular reason' (*TST*, p. 263). Gerard Loughlin, one of the contributors to *Radical Orthodoxy*, earlier wrote a substantial book on narrative theology, from which the title of this chapter is taken.[7]

So far, so good. But Milbank is not content with the *general* idea of narrative as an alternative to secular reason. This is his main disagreement with MacIntyre, and where we see Radical Orthodoxy staking out its own ground (*TST*, p. 262). Radical Orthodoxy demands a specific commitment to the Chris-

tian story *alone* as the way to combat nihilism. Going back to
story, myth and tradition is not enough. A plurality of stories can't
stem the tide of the secular. In fact, capitalism is quite happy for
lots of religious positions to jostle together and compete. It's all
part of the marketplace, it adds variety. And variety is the spice
of life.

Not so, argues Milbank. Variety can be meaningless and
empty, like endlessly flicking through the hundreds of satellite
TV channels without ever choosing anything. That kind of variety simply hides us from the fact that, for all this choice, nothing
is really different, nothing really stands out. In the sweet shop,
it doesn't matter what we select. It's arbitrary. And so Radical
Orthodoxy, accepting that there are no universal rational foundations, accepting that Christianity will be seen by many as just
one story among others, still insists on taking this stand on 'the
plain unfounded narrative of Christianity which is the only
"universal" for those who situate themselves within it' (*TST*,
p. 173). The story invites us to become part of it, to become insiders. Secular reason 'cannot be refuted, but only out-narrated,
if we can *persuade* people – for reasons of "literary taste" – that
Christianity offers a much better story' (*TST*, p. 330).

This is not just another story, but the only one which can make
our choices meaningful. Radical Orthodoxy takes a strange path,
through scepticism and stories to the assertion that Christian
theology is supreme. And the only grounds for sharing its jour-
ney are those of 'literary taste'. Is this enough?

We should not assume that this appeal to literary taste is anything to do with polite middle-class book circles swapping tea,
chardonnay and gossip over the latest Muriel Spark novel. It is
combative, uncompromising and rude. What is it that motivates
this forceful stance? The claim is this: Christianity must seek to
master and defeat all other stories, because it is the only story which
is able to renounce mastery and domination. In the end, only
Christianity can tell a story about everything which is at the same
time a story of peace. And it can do this because those who tell
the Christian story participate in the mind of God. Their reason
is not unaided secular universalism. It is a vision lit up by the

divine light. The Christian has reasons of which the non-Christian knows nothing.

Remember that Milbank objects to the idea that stories or traditions in general are a 'good thing'. And so Christianity's unique story must be affirmed. His claim is that 'Christianity is unique in refusing ultimate reality to all conflictual phenomena' (*TST*, p. 262). This goes beyond secularism, which is only the latest version of pagan thinking. In the end, Radical Orthodoxy is asking us to believe that, apart from Christianity, all other stories about the world give first place to chaos, violence and brute power. Even when those stories proclaim mercy and peace, they are reacting against this evil reality.[8]

The shape of Radical Orthodoxy's story is becoming a little clearer. It welcomes postmodernism as its chance to undermine the universal claims of secular reason. It welcomes the renewed emphasis on story, community and virtue found among the postliberals. It claims no foundation for the truth of Christianity beyond the compelling beauty of the story and the vision it sustains. But because Christianity is a story of ultimate peace and harmony between all differences that make up creation, it escapes the net of sceptical postmodernism.

How? Milbank argues that relativism is itself just another story. Saying that there is no ultimate truth is itself a claim about ultimate truth. Some kind of big story, some vision of ultimate truth is unavoidable. Postmodernism turns difference into fragmentation and conflict, but there is no reason why we are forced to accept this viewpoint. Consider this statement by Milbank (in which 'perspectivism' is another way of talking about relativism):

> Christianity is quite unable to refute rationally the ontology of difference, or the thought of mastery. Nevertheless, it is uniquely able to reveal this doctrine of perspectivism as itself just another perspective: the perspective of a paganism made aware of its worship of violence by Christianity, and then nakedly espousing such worship. (*TST*, p. 262)

Radical Orthodoxy looks at the differences that make up the world and sees in them 'the concealed text of an original peaceful creation' (*TST*, p. 417). The Christian God is the Trinity, difference in harmony – and all creation is called to share in that harmony. The infinite differences that make up creation can be in harmony because 'there are no substances in creation'. Everything is interconnected, everything is made up of relationships and so everything reflects the nature of God and can participate in God (*TST*, pp. 424–5). The postmodern view of language as a system of differences is taken up by Radical Orthodoxy as an image of creation itself. Graham Ward – who welcomes Derrida's views on difference and language – states both that Christ's identity can never be fixed and, nevertheless, that Christ is a controlling sign, and only in relation to him do any other signs become theologically meaningful.[9]

Milbank himself offers perhaps the best summary of our discussion so far:

> Theology purports to give an ultimate narrative, to provide some ultimate depth of description, because the situation of oneself within such a narrative is what it means to belong to the Church, to be a Christian. However, the claim is made by faith, not a reason which seeks foundations. (*TST*, p. 249)

However, this raises a question. If narrative is everything, what is the point of *Theology and Social Theory*, and, indeed, all the other publications for which Radical Orthodoxy has been responsible? Why not simply preach the gospel, read the scriptures, celebrate the sacraments? Why all this extra verbiage?

This leads us into the heart of a tension within Radical Orthodoxy. If the Christian story is enough, then why bother with Radical Orthodoxy? If, however, Radical Orthodoxy (or any theology) does have a role, doesn't this mean that the Christian story needs propping up with external supports?

This second option threatens to bring the project crashing down. Milbank is clear that one must be inside the Christian story, and that to be inside it is to refuse any external voice of criticism: 'what Christians claim to be unique about the Christian text is that it ultimately withstands all criticism to such a degree that our understanding must remain within the confines of interpretation in relation to it' (*WMS*, p. 140).

What is the Christian 'text'? Milbank seems to be referring to Christ as presented in the scriptures and sacraments. The story of Christ – and the way that story is retold and performed by the Church – seems to be enough. But Milbank is well aware that the Church has done more than add footnotes to the Bible or to the Gospels. It has added new dimensions to the original story.

Milbank writes that 'Narratives only identify God because they simultaneously invent the unpresentable idea of God' (*TST*, p. 385). In other words, story alone is not enough. The story points beyond itself to a reality of God which no language can capture. And this leads to uncertainty about what the story means. This is why the Church produces doctrines, or official teachings. These teachings bring out what is implied by the story. But they also add a new dimension. The fully worked-out orthodox doctrines of the divine and human natures of Christ, or of the Trinity, are not logically demanded by scripture. They are made up by the Church (in Milbank's words, there is a 'radically "inventive"' and 'ungrounded' addition) to clear up questions which the story and Christian living don't decide on their own (*TST*, p. 384).

This is why Milbank objects to George Lindbeck's theology. Remember that MacIntyre was taken to task for supposedly putting his faith in a general idea of 'tradition', which could be used to understand different stories and practices. Milbank objected that Christian theology demanded faith in the uniqueness of its own story. A similar point is made against Lindbeck, who is accused of having a timeless, rigid idea of 'narrative' which is then applied to Christianity. Milbank calls this 'a new narratological foundationalism' which 'fails to arrive at a postmodern theology'. In other words, Lindbeck is not postliberal and postmodern enough. He has smuggled in the idea of 'story' as the new universal foundation on which to build truth.

For Milbank, this is not radical enough. He wants the Christian story to be open to genuinely new insights. History is never over and done. But to preserve the orthodoxy of this position, the Church must be given a decisive role in working out which new insights are valid additions and which are not. The Church, as we will see in the next chapter, becomes a virtual extension of the incarnation of God in Christ. As Milbank says, 'the metanarrative is not just the story of Jesus, it is the continuing story of the Church' (*TST*, p. 387).

The metanarrative – the big, overarching Christian story – is a story of everything, centred on Christ. But it seems to depend entirely on the Church. With no rational foundations to appeal to, is it based on anything more than the arbitrary authority of a flawed human institution which claims to be divine? Does it put the Church in the place of Christ?

The answer must have something to do with the special power of the Church's language, a power to shape reality which no other language can exercise without doing violence to the world. For Pickstock, that power is seen most clearly in the Church's celebration of the Eucharist. Are there some clues here to help us understand more clearly the paradoxes of Radical Orthodoxy?

Seeing is believing: why symbols aren't enough

Radical Orthodoxy offers a kind of postmodern theology. It celebrates differences, bodies and the open-endedness of time. In the same breath, it wants to gather all these things into a single story of harmonious peace. Language gives way to something immediate.

Stephen Long is a good example of this. One of the problems with modern liberal theology, he believes, is that it has been too modest in its claims. Theologians like Paul Tillich developed a theory of the symbolic nature of all talk about God. Tillich argued that symbols, unlike ordinary signs, actually participate in the reality they represent. They express the nature of divine reality. At the same time, symbols are limited and inadequate. Something of God always escapes them.

According to Long, both sides of this theory are flawed. The idea that symbols participate in God's nature might sound close to Radical Orthodoxy. But Long says that in its liberal version, this leads to the view that all religious symbols, across different traditions, are straightforwardly hooked up to God. This denies the specific nature of the Christian faith. And it's made worse by the admission that symbols are inadequate and limited, because this drains Christianity of its absolute claims.

Long believes that Christian language *is* adequate to God. As a result, he dismisses the idea that the Church and its claims must be subjected to criticism and constant reform. If we tried fundamentally to reform the Church, we would be claiming that we stood on a higher moral and spiritual ground. But there is no such ground outside the Church. In the context of Long's discussion of economic theory, we are faced with an either/or: '*either* the church and its spokespersons *or* the contemporary market and its spokespersons must finally persuade us' (*DE*, p. 230).

Remember that Long's objection to contemporary economic theory was that it assumed we started from a situation of scarcity. He applies this point to liberal views of the limitations of theological language. If we assume that theology's words are limited, then whatever we say will be a betrayal of God: 'To speak of God is to speak against God.' The apparent humility and modesty of liberal theology is a conceit. How do liberals know that our words about God are inadequate? Only, Long argues, if they 'implicitly claim to know the *more* that cannot be named' (*DE*, p. 264). In other words, liberal theologians are expecting us to believe that they can stand outside the Church and the Church's language about God, and check out just how well it represents God. And then they can descend from the dizzy heights and tell us poor mortals that our language falls short.

Long's alternative is that we accept that God gives us a fullness of language to speak God's name. And this means that we accept that the Church is the institution which polices and directs that language. The clear implication seems to be that the Church must be infallible in order that its language about God defies all criticism. Long is certainly scathing about the 'Protestant principle' that just because the Church is historical it must therefore be fallible. Accepting that the Church can be mistaken, Long argues, means that other institutions and practices will define the truth.

Long has put his finger on a key element of Enlightenment thinking which is rejected by Radical Orthodoxy: its epistemology, that is, its theory of how we know anything, what kind of knowledge we have and how we justify it. Philip Blond has particularly targeted this aspect of modernity.

Just as Long takes on the modern split between facts and values, Blond attacks the division between reality and appearances. As we have seen, Kant argued that we do not know things as they are in themselves. We only have access to appearances. For Blond, this leads us to a disastrous schizophrenia. Finite beings are cut off from their transcendent divine source. They become brute things. And the ideal and infinite becomes a dreamy, abstract nothingness, for ever separated from the world we touch and taste.

The way we understand language is part of the problem for Blond. It can become 'disembodied' – a collection of concepts cut off from the world, imposing order on the formless void of things. He sees the roots of this modern split in the theory of nominalism. Again, Duns Scotus is largely to blame for this, though others such as William of Ockham are also hauled over the coals. Nominalism denied that the universal terms of language had any real existence 'out there'. Language was cut off from reality. This pulled the rug from under the analogical view of the world which had established a real relationship between the world and God, without denying God's difference.

Once it was accepted that the being of the world and the being of God were essentially the same, the die was cast. God was no longer different in kind from us, and could only be distinguished by his infinite power: 'man could see God only as a greater and more powerful version of himself' (*RONT*, p. 233). God is hidden, and is made known only by the arbitrary exercise of his will. Human knowledge becomes deprived of divine illumination and certainty. It was only a matter of time before, exhausted by this indecision, modernity abolished God altogether and claimed his power for itself.

The solution is to reconnect signs and things, to realize that we can *see* the truth and beauty of God in the world around us. As we see it, so we can share in it, and become true and beautiful ourselves (*PSP*, p. 57). This is supremely revealed by Christ, the Word made flesh, who again makes visible the invisible.

This separation between words and things is a theme running through a number of Radical Orthodox writings. John Montag also blames developments rooted in Duns Scotus' thought for a situation in which 'language cannot but mask reality' (*RONT*, p. 51) and calls for 'a reversal of the "divorce between words and things"' (*RONT*, p. 58). Too much modern theology divorces God's revelation from our faithful response, but this is a false separation. Revelation *is* the establishment of a relationship with God, not a body of dogmatic information which is external to us.

In his essay in the same collection, Conor Cunningham welcomes Wittgenstein's attempt to free us from other-worldly philosophical explanations, returning language to life. But Wittgenstein is still criticized, because he does not have an explicitly theological account of language. He is forced to look for a definition of reality in purely this-worldly terms. And this becomes another abstract foundation, which saps language, time and matter of their life. Cunningham ends with a familiar point: making the transcendent into something ineffable and beyond language is wrong. It turns the transcendent into an ineffective ghostly nothing ('Such a transcendent cannot really make a difference to finite reality' (*RONT*, p. 86)) and makes language and time irrelevant things we need to escape.

Radical Orthodoxy once again sets a definite commitment to Christian theology against all alternatives: 'By contrast, only a grounding in a transcendent source which expresses itself in a specific language saves the ultimacy of language. Only for theology, not philosophy, is grammar the last word' (*RONT*, p. 86). In other words, theology alone is committed to a specific community, story and guiding rules, which show us how to speak of God and the world together.

The attack on the secular is therefore intimately bound up with this theological account of language, the world and God. To see how this all hangs together, it is worth quoting Blond at length:

There is no such thing as a secular realm, a part of the world that can be elevated above God and explained and investigated apart from him. This means that the world can only be understood in its relationship to God, and God can (from *our* perspective and not in himself) be only understood in terms of his relationship to the world . . . [I]t is worldly form as God-given (culminated and expressed in the union of word and flesh in Christ) that is revelatory, and nothing else. For there is no division between grace and nature, no separation of revelation from all of creation, and, consequently, no possible denial that the world shows and exhibits its participation in universal theological forms that can and must be seen.   (*RONT*, p. 235)

This is vintage Radical Orthodoxy: it is anti-secular because it wants to redeem the *world* as the place where God is revealed. It is also very sure of itself. Blond is clear that 'only theology can, in the fullest sense of the word, *see* at all' (*RONT*, p. 232). It is 'only Christian theology that teaches us that the visible world is for us' (*RONT*, p. 240). Although Blond is clear that there is always more to see, that God's reality is not exhausted by the world, it seems that only Christians can truly perceive this.

If we are to understand a little more of why Radical Orthodoxy takes this stance, we need to turn our attention in more detail to that 'proper word' for God: Jesus Christ.

The poetic Christ or Christ the poem?

In James Smith's extended account of language from a Radical Orthodox perspective, *Speech and Theology*, it is striking that the central idea is that of incarnation. He begins by asking whether all conceptual language is violent, because it tries to grasp and contain what should be other and transcendent. Our lived experience, other people and God – these realities can't be caught in words without doing some violence to their nature, their otherness.

As an alternative to this grasping way of using language, Smith puts forward an incarnational approach. This is based on the nature of Christ, the Word become flesh. Christ, as divine, remains transcendent, but appears in the world. The divine and the human are not confused or identified, but nor are they divorced from one another.

Taking his cue from Augustine, Smith argues that an incarnational view of language can be seen in activities such as praise and confession. Praise allows us to speak of God without reducing God to a thing we can grasp and manipulate. Instead, it affirms God's transcendence, and draws us into an experience of God (*ST*, p. 128). Confession enables us to express ourselves, without reducing our intimate selves to objects.

The 'incarnational logic' of these ways of speaking rescues us from violating God's otherness or else admitting defeat and withdrawing into total silence, neither of which is able to redeem the world and resist the forces of violence. In the incarnation, God is revealed under historical conditions, as a fully human being, and this is the only way (Smith argues) in which we could receive God's revelation. Revelation that drops down from heaven with no regard for our human ways of knowing and experiencing would just pass us by. We'd have no way of encountering it (*ST*, pp. 166–7).

The implication of all this is that language is not just a tool for labelling things in the world. It is a medium of relationship. God is both present and absent in the world. The job of language is to relate us to God, to make the experience of God possible as God is revealed to us, without pretending that we have got God in our grip.

The incarnation is not an isolated historical event. It shows us how God is revealed in the creation and in the life of faith. God gives himself to us in relationship, and does so in a worldly, embodied way, without losing his essential otherness. Smith can therefore make the bigger claim that the logic of incarnation 'is the condition of possibility of revelation and hence the condition of possibility of language, which is itself a donation [i.e. something given by God]' (*ST*, p. 176).

This brings us back to the point where we started: Pickstock's grand statement about the Eucharist being the condition of possibility for all meaning. We will look more fully at Radical Orthodoxy's view of Church and Eucharist in the next chapter.

For now, it is worth tracing the bare outlines of Pickstock's argument.

The first part of *After Writing* contains her version of the attack on secular modernity, what she calls 'the polity of death'. The modern age, she claims, is in love with death. One of the thinkers she takes as representative of this is Derrida. This might at first seem odd, since Derrida, as we have seen, was also a critic of modernity's ambitions to secure absolute foundations for truth. For Pickstock, however, Derrida's thought remains stuck in the modern groove. This is mainly due to his view of language.

Derrida argued that philosophy's obsession with certainty and self-evident truth has to do with its suppression of writing. Philosophy prefers the spoken word as its model of language, because the speaker is supposedly directly present in his or her words. Writing can be deceptive, because it can become detached from its author and its context and its subject matter. Writing is a symptom of language detached from reality. Speech is direct and immediate. It is *present*.

Derrida turned this around and asked, what if we started with writing? Writing, by its nature, invites different interpretations, and there is no authority in the text itself which can decide the ultimate correctness of these variations. Writing shows us that language is a system of differences, of traces, in which a full, absolute present truth – a truth which is simply and obviously *there* – never arrives.

Some have greeted Derrida's insight as a liberation of philosophy from illusory dreams of presence, and authoritarian attempts to fix truth. But Pickstock turns the tables on him. She argues that the reason speech was so highly valued by ancient philosophers was that it emphasizes the living, relational nature of communication. For Socrates, we discover truth only through the cut and thrust of dialogue. This is a defence against the temptation to turn language into a commodity, as when Socrates' opponents the sophists simply used words as decorative rhetoric to gain power over their listeners. And speech was related most closely to worship, to that relationship to the true Good which was about praise and participation, not ownership. So speech wasn't to be used to tie down the true and divine, but to set us free for a non-possessive relationship with them.

Set against this backdrop, Derrida's turn to writing looks very different. Writing, for Pickstock, is something we have in our grasp. We look down on a page of text. It is disembodied, torn away from a living relationship with speaking subjects. It is open to our control and manipulation. It occupies space, rather than time.

Writing and modernity, she argues, go hand in hand. The modern secular age dreams of a space which it can survey in a glance, comprehend and control. It turns creation into a space of dead objects, things we can use and abuse at will. It is like English philosopher Jeremy Bentham's (1748–1832) 'panopticon', the fantasy prison in which all the inmates were permanently under surveillance from a central point. Far from being liberating, Derrida's version of postmodernism is the flip-side of naked capitalism and crushing dictatorship.

So Pickstock seeks to recover a sense of language as liturgy, as worship directed towards our sharing in the divine nature. 'Truth' becomes an event, a relationship in time, sustained in a community's worship. It is supremely encountered and received in the Eucharist, the Christian sacrament in which Christ becomes present in bread and wine. As with the incarnation itself, in the Eucharist, the infinite and divine is revealed in a worldly, embodied, timely form.

For Pickstock, the Church is brought into being in and through its receiving of the Eucharist. Although secularism is her principal enemy, she is clear that developments within Christianity also undermined this mutual relationship. Duns Scotus gets a hard time again for making God's being and ours the same (univocal) while making God more and more detached and unknowable. The eucharistic link between God and humanity is undermined by this. In the Reformation, neither Protestants nor Catholics managed to keep hold of the balance. Protestants turned the bread and wine into mere signs, detached from Christ's reality. Catholics put such stress on the sacrament as the body of Christ that they neglected the truth that the community of the Church was Christ's body too.

According to Pickstock, a true appreciation of the Eucharist is vital for a number of reasons:

- It restores the primary purpose of language as worship of God.
- It shows how God is revealed in the world in a way that establishes and confirms a real relationship between the infinite and the finite. It shows us that 'being is that which is always already relational' (*AW*, p. 248).
- It shows how created things and signs are not doomed to be dead objects, but can be part of a living response to God. It gets round all of modern and postmodern contradictions between presence and absence, life and death, worldly and other-worldly.
- It shows us how the incarnation of God in Christ is received and continued in community, in the Church's reception of the Eucharist.

Why, though, does Pickstock take the Latin Mass as her ideal example of how the Eucharist achieves all of these things?

One reason is that it is full of stops and starts. It doesn't have a straightforward, linear structure. And this means it jolts us out of the mundane, secular world into a dynamic relationship with God. As we take part in it, our identity is reshaped and we are opened out to God. Our giving is taken up into the life of the giving God, into the life of the Trinity.

But there is another factor that makes the Latin Mass so important: it is associated with transubstantiation. This is the doctrine that, in some way, the bread and wine actually become the body and blood of Christ. Remember that Radical Orthodoxy wants to heal the split between words and things. Well here, in the Eucharist, that division is completely overcome.

Transubstantiation might sound like a very speculative and abstract doctrine, but Pickstock disagrees. Liberal ideas of how language about God works – as symbols which are detached and inadequate – leave us cut off from God, and they reduce language to a string of dead and empty signs. Transubstantiation makes signs into living connections with God once again. And it restores us to a true appreciation of time, the physical world and language itself. The Eucharist shows that there is an incarnational dimension to all language. It 'allows *all* signs to become concelebration' (*AW*, p. 258). Concelebration refers to the liturgical practice when a number of priests share together in the prayer of thanksgiving over the bread and wine. It is an image of the communal nature of priesthood. Pickstock is suggesting that this sacred, sacramental reality is not confined to specifically ecclesial language and rituals, but reveals something of the true nature of all communication. Any word can mediate the presence of God. The Eucharist therefore doesn't separate us from the world and signs, it 'situates us more inside language than ever' (*AW*, p. 262). It makes it possible for us to trust signs again.

If the Eucharist is so important, what has happened to Christ? Pickstock would argue that, because we live in time, we receive Christ again and again. This is the nature of the divine gift – it is always repeated in new ways. There is no one absolute starting point. Pickstock writes that the Eucharist 'repeats Christ as Himself always nothing other than the gift of the Eucharist' (*AW*, p. 264).

There is something highly ambiguous about what Pickstock is saying here. On one interpretation, Christ seems to be nothing more than what happens when the Church gathers. And this threatens to drain Christ of any specific significance. Would it matter, for example, if the historical Jesus never actually existed?

It seems that the only way to overcome the split between language and things is to make everything into a sign. From Radical Orthodoxy's point of view, this is a good thing, because it reminds us that everything only has being because it is grounded in and directs us to God the Giver. But this makes its claims highly questionable. It is not clear which comes first: Jesus and the specific content of the Christian story; or a general theory about signs and how they work. And there is no way of judging this, because once the gap between signs and things is sealed up, there is no way of offering any criticism of a text. It just is what it is. But why couldn't *any* movement claim that its rituals and words were identical with things?

It is not even clear that Radical Orthodoxy is consistent on this point. Although many of its authors decry the split between words and things, they still admit that God cannot just be represented in words. There is always something more to God and something new to be revealed. If this is the case, then language is still inadequate. Even if we accept that language isn't just descriptive, but brings us into a living relationship with the world, others and God, it is a big leap from this to claiming that language can create perfect relationships.

The logic of arguments like Pickstock's and Long's appears to be that if we admit any uncertainty about what signs refer to, or if we admit that they might be imperfect, then we are doomed to be utterly lost, lovers of dead things. Their solution is to take certain signs, claim that they offer us absolutely reliable access to God, and conclude that this shows us what all language should be like. But both the diagnosis and the cure proposed make huge assumptions. Why should there be an either/or: either transubstantiation or nihilism? Either the Church is infallible, or it possesses no truth at all?

We might begin to suspect that behind Radical Orthodoxy's criticism of modernity lies a very modern desire for absolute certainty. Behind its attempt to give worth back to the created world lies the very abstract idea that accepting a certain theory about signs is necessary for anything to mean anything. Milbank might claim that 'language is also "like God" and our linguistic expression mirrors the divine creative act' (*WMS*, p. 29), but what is reflected in a mirror is never identical to the original. Its exact form depends on the physical qualities of the mirror and the angle of reflection.

More importantly, our use of language is itself shaped by culture, history, politics and so on. As we will see, when Radical Orthodoxy talks about the Church in positive terms, for example, it is hard to know exactly what it is referring to. An ideal? But this would mean that the ideal was separate from the actual churches we see around us. Or is it saying that the Church as we know it in history is already the ideal? But then, which church, in which period of history? And what do we do about those awkward facts about the Church's involvement in error, corruption and violence? Pickstock's Latin Mass seems to float above all history. It is an abstraction, quite divorced from the power relations that would have shaped its actual performance at any one time and place.

The concern about where this leaves the historical Jesus has even been picked up by insiders to the fold. Stephen Long has noted that 'Milbank does appear to eviscerate Jesus of any substantial content' (*DE*, p. 251). He is referring particularly to Milbank's essays on Jesus in *The Word Made Strange*. They begin with a general discussion of human poetic existence. This does not just refer to poetry in the narrow sense, but the ancient idea of *poesis*, which includes all creative activity.

Milbank argues that human beings are always trying to make meaningful objects. But the meaning those objects have is never entirely predictable. The things we make take on significance beyond our original intentions. We can receive them back again as gifts, offering new meanings to us. Milbank takes this to be an image of how revelation works. Revelation is not something totally alien to us, but nor is it only a projection of human aspirations onto the heavens. Rather, God, of his own free will, meets us in and through the things we make: 'revelation itself may be defined as the intersection of the divine and human creations' (*WMS*, p. 130).

Poetry – in this sense of creative activity – shapes our imagination of what life should be like by creating what Milbank calls 'concrete universals'. These are pictures and stories which provide a standard and a purpose against which we judge our actual life. For example, Homer's epics gave his listeners images of virtue and honour which helped them to work out where they stood, and what kind of people they should become.

According to Milbank, the Old Testament is in search of such poetic images and stories for how Israel should relate to God. This search is only fulfilled in the New Testament. Jesus, the Word made flesh, brings together the divine and human creations. All other pictures were limited. Only in Jesus is the image totally adequate to God. And only in Jesus do we get a definitive picture of what the human response to God should be: 'Christ is our proper word for God and for true humanity' (*WMS*, p. 140). This has an important implication. Only in the light of Christ do we know what goodness, sin, love and justice are. Christ comes first, not abstract ideas of morality, or nature, or law.

Is Christ, however, just an image or ideal? How does Christ make a difference to us? Traditionally, the doctrine of the atonement has tried to answer this, by arguing in different ways that Christ was our representative, that he offered himself in our place on the cross. Milbank takes up this teaching, but adds a twist. It's a twist that takes some work to follow.

According to Pickstock, modernity is in love with death. Its language is cut off from the living world, a collection of dead and empty signs. Radical Orthodoxy wants to bring language and things, language and life back together again. A first step is to see language itself as dynamic, made up of relationships, its meanings defined by the living use words are put to by a community. A second step is to understand that language shows us what the world is like. Creation too is made up of relationships, not fixed substances.

With this understanding of language and the world in place, we can approach the meaning of Jesus, and specifically of the atonement. Milbank says that signs work because they are lifeless: 'our signs speak only death' (*WMS*, p. 139). How can signs be saved, and death overcome? Only if God in Christ becomes a sign for us, taking upon himself all death, all misrepresentation, all failed communication, and then translating all of this into the fullness of new life, of relationship restored, of meaning fulfilled.

All language, Milbank argues, is metaphorical. All signs are 'substitutes'. They have meaning only in relation to other signs. Christ becomes a sign, becomes part of language, but does not leave it dead and cut off from the world. He accepts death and disfigurement as part of his meaning, but his response is one of peace. He forgives, he is non-violent. He becomes the ultimate sign, the ultimate metaphor, the ultimate figure who substitutes his life-giving peace for our distorted constructions of meaning and power.

Christ is therefore the true fulfilment of all human poetry, of every attempt we make to give meaning to our lives. This is why, as we saw, Milbank claims that the 'Christian text withstands all criticism'. We only know true meaning because of Christ. There is no way of standing apart from Christ and seeing the truth, because that would mean we were still stuck with lifeless signs, and an unhealed world of resentment.

To understand this intricate interpretation, it helps to see how Milbank distinguishes it from the accounts he rejects:

- Liberals want to strip away all the mythical elements from the Gospels, leaving a purely historical account of Jesus. The problem here is that there is no such thing as 'pure' history. It is always interpreted. And the idea that history has to exclude myth and any reference to the transcendent is a secular prejudice. In any case, it is well known that accounts of the 'historical Jesus' are often coloured by the limited cultural assumptions of the historian.
- Conservatives want to begin with timeless revealed beliefs (the doctrines of the atonement or the incarnation) as the key to Jesus' identity. However, this means that history is not taken seriously, and the doctrines of the Church are imposed on reality from the outside. Milbank is bracing in his rejection of this second option: 'it is pointless to approach incarnation and atonement primarily as revealed propositions' (*WMS*, p. 148). We need to understand what difference they make to us.

Narrative theology tries to avoid the problems of liberals and conservatives, both of whom sacrifice the actual gospel story to abstract ideas of history or revelation. Narrative theologians ask us to begin with the gospel stories to find out what Jesus' character is. The doctrine of the incarnation isn't separated from the stories, because 'The character of Jesus, as it emerges in this story, is a supreme pointer to the character of God himself' (*WMS*, p. 149). The Gospels therefore give concrete content to belief in Jesus. We might think that Milbank would endorse this view. But he takes a surprising turn.

Milbank argues that the Gospels don't reveal Jesus' character, his inner psychology, his personality development. They point to his works, what he does, as evidence of his universal significance. When they talk about his identity, it is in poetic images which are very general (word, truth, bread, life, etc.). And by identifying him with God, they 'evacuate' Jesus of any particular identifiable content.

This is necessary, because Jesus has to point to the beginning and the end of all things, to the horizon in which all human meaning is worked out. All that is specific is erased, and all that is left is the proper name 'Jesus'. And Milbank recognizes that there is a paradox here. The more Jesus is talked about as the incarnation of God, the more he becomes 'disincarnate', an abstraction who adds nothing specific to our knowledge of God (*WMS*, p. 150). In the introduction to *The Word Made Strange*, Milbank affirms that 'Jesus is essentially a linguistic and poetic reality' (*WMS*, p. 3). Has Jesus – and orthodoxy, for that matter – been dissolved into human language and the postmodern play of signs?

This is the root of Long's worry that Milbank is guilty of 'eviscerating' Jesus of any substance. As we know, however, Milbank can quite cheerfully throw out the idea of fixed and time-less substances and identities. Everything is in flux. Why not Jesus?

The question remains, however. If Jesus is nothing more than a name, why bother with him at all? Milbank offers two related answers:

- 'The gospels can be read, not as the story of Jesus, but as the story of the (re)foundation of a new city, a new kind of human community, Israel-become-the-Church. Jesus figures in this story simply as the founder, the beginning, the first of many' (*WMS*, p. 150). Here we see again the importance of the Church as the body of Christ, the community which is effect-ively an extension of the incarnation through history. This community is necessary. It puts into practice forgiveness and reconciliation, without which Christianity would just be a collection of abstract 'beliefs', and Jesus would just be a good man stuck in the past, or a divine saviour stuck in heaven.

- The second answer backtracks a little, and does give Jesus some specific content again. As we've seen, it is central to Milbank's idea of the atonement that Jesus offers a non-violent response to abuse and death and so becomes a sign of life for us. So the stress on the founding of the Church is held together with the belief that the Church is for ever patterned on Jesus' response: 'In Jesus we see the perfect "shape" of forgiveness, and this inaugurates a new form of association which aims to be based on such a practice' (*WMS*, p. 164).

For Jesus to be significant for us, these two things have to be held together. First, Jesus needs to become a liberating sign: 'on the cross . . . Jesus is "substituted" for us because here (as the accounts of the last supper suggest) he becomes totally a sign, here he is transformed into a perfect metaphor of forgiveness' (*WMS*, p. 160). Second, this sign then needs to be realized, lived out by a community, by the Church: 'The most concrete elements in the gospels are the general injunctions and examples regarding Christian practice. Only here do we "identify" God incarnate, and this identification should be fleshed out in the later history and contemporary life of the Church' (*WMS*, p. 165).

The concern highlighted by Long still remains, however. If Jesus is no more than a 'perfect metaphor', and if the Church is the community where forgiveness really happens, do we really need to maintain the pretence that the Gospels have any historical reality at all? Can't we just admit that Jesus ('an essentially linguistic and poetic reality') is an invention of the Church, a symbol we have made up to help us imagine what forgiveness and true reconciliation are like?

Milbank would not accept this criticism. Remember that he sees revelation as the coming together of human and divine creativity. The fact that human beings, or the Church in particular, might have 'invented' Jesus' story and the teachings about him does not mean that they are not also given to us by God. God is revealed in the things we make. That doesn't make God (or Christ) into our creation. But it does mean that our making is a necessary part of revelation. What we make, we experience as a gift. Christ is both a given, and 'still being given, re-born, through our own spirit-inspired constructions' (*WMS*, p. 142).

Milbank seeks to overcome dualisms between nature and grace, faith and reason, divine and human creativity. However, the question of 'orthodoxy' still haunts this account. A claim to authority is being asserted. It is as if, for all its desire to avoid dualism, Radical Orthodoxy still needs to appeal to a *deus ex machina*, a God from outside the world, who steps in to prevent the signs and stories of the Church being read as just more human words. There is a doctrine of inspiration at work, here, but it is far from clear how it works. What are the criteria for recognizing that something is spirit-inspired and not merely wilful?

Graham Ward takes this interpretation of Christ further in his *Cities of God*. In the second part of that book, 'The Analogical World View', Ward underlines the links we have already traced between Radical Orthodoxy's critique of secular modernity, its view of language, and its interpretation of the incarnation and the Church.

Ward begins by talking about the scandal contained in Jesus' words 'This is my body'. According to logic, Jesus is talking nonsense. And this is supported by modern ideas of knowledge. In modernity, reality consists of objects which are available to observation. Each object is what it is, and language simply labels objects: 'this is a chair'.

For Ward, Jesus' words undermine this stable, self-contained modern view. They suggest that the identity of things and people and meanings is not so static, obvious and open to view. Matter and bodies are not fixed and absolute. They are created and so they are linked by analogy with the divine and with one another. Bodies are 'not autonomous and self-defining, but sharing and being shared' (*CG*, p. 91). They are always communicating, giving and receiving signs, although importantly Ward does not simply identify bodies with signs, as he is wary of individual bodies simply being wished away or disappeared, merged into a larger whole.

The true nature of our bodies is revealed by the body of Christ, which is a body that is always being displaced. The body is living, dead, resurrected, ascended. It is in a particular place, but it is universal. It is given and received in the Eucharist. It becomes a community in the Church. As Milbank and Pickstock say that Jesus is the sign that makes all other signs meaningful, Ward argues that Christ's body 'is the true body and all these other bodies become true only in their participation within Christ's body'. He goes on to say that 'Christ's body is the pure sign – the only sign that is self-defining' (*CG*, p. 93).

Bodies are redeemed by their relationship with the body of Christ as a life-giving body, made available in the Eucharist and the Church. Ward's (often beautiful) meditation on 'The Displaced Body of Jesus Christ' attempts to show how the instability of Jesus' body allows Christ to cross boundaries such as gender, ethnicity and, ultimately, that between life and death. Jesus is handed over, broken and consumed, lost and recovered. The cross makes possible the resurrection, as 'Christ's withdrawal of his body makes possible a greater identification with that body' (*CG*, p. 108). The body/sign of Christ does not stay with death. It is 'disseminated in "new languages of the Gospel"' (*CG*, p. 110).

Ward reminds us of the threads which run through our discussion so far.

- On a secular and pagan view, language is a collection of dead signs that corresponds to a world of lifeless objects – playthings of power or commodities in the marketplace.
- On a Christian view, language is made up of differences and relationships which can be brought into harmony. And the gap between language and the world needs to be healed. The world itself is, like language, made out of relationships, not fixed substances.
- This general view of language actually springs from the specific Christian belief that Jesus Christ is the Word of God. In our view of God and humanity, Jesus is the final word, sign, image, metaphor.
- Jesus' identity is not static. It is a sign taken up into the Church, handed over to the community which practises the way of life Jesus offered.

Language, creation, incarnation, Eucharist, Church – everything is interrelated: 'Communication confers communion and creates community' (*CG*, p. 111).

Faced by this web of shifting relationships, how does Radical Orthodoxy stop itself becoming another version of relativism? What distinguishes it from sceptical postmodernism? Radical Orthodoxy undoubtedly does seek anchors. Pickstock looks to the Eucharist as the perfect communication of God's presence. Milbank makes the name of Jesus unique and the community which he founded absolute. Ward writes of Christ as the only 'self-defining' sign.

The question is: can these anchors really do the job they are called on to do? Can they really free us from the uncertainties of scepticism? Do they run the risk of turning the stories and beliefs of Christianity into abstractions, lifeless verbiage that makes no real difference to the world?

Every time this question is raised, one thing becomes clear. It is the question of the Church that is crucial. Unless the Church really can be the place where the bread and wine become Christ's body and blood, where forgiveness creates real community and where the union of God and humanity is brought about, then we might have to break out the lifebelts. Because without the Church, Radical Orthodoxy is all at sea.

Chapter summary

- Language is one of the central concerns of modern philosophy. The way language shapes and orders the world can no longer be ignored.
- Along with this centrality of language comes an anxiety: perhaps language is cut off from reality, or distorts it?
- Radical Orthodoxy criticizes the typical modern view of language as something separated from reality and from the transcendent which gives depth to that reality.
- It unifies language and reality. Creation is something like a language, and mirrors the nature of God. Our poetic creativity becomes the means by which we encounter revelation.

- Truth is story-shaped. We have to be part of the community that tells the right story about God, i.e. the Church. But there is no way of justifying this on secular rational grounds. Only the aesthetics, the brilliance of the story can persuade us.
- The story is experienced supremely in the Eucharist, where the gap between sign and reality is overcome in the bread and wine which are the body and blood of Christ.
- Christ himself becomes a sign, a metaphor of forgiveness and the name of one who founded the community where the story of reconciliation is continued, celebrated and practised.
- We have asked whether it is credible to equate one story with reality in this way, thereby excluding all rational criticism that is not already lit up by the story. We have also considered the way in which the Eucharist can be made into a timeless abstraction, and Jesus emptied of historical content. Do these concerns cast doubt on whether Radical Orthodoxy makes good on its intentions?

2

Community:
the all-consuming Church

Language is not spoken in a vacuum. It shapes, and is shaped in turn, by historical, social and cultural relationships.

Radical Orthodoxy accepts that meaningful communication happens in a context. Its distinctive claim is that only in the Church can we find the context in which true words of God can be received and spoken. Outside of that setting, community breaks down and language becomes just another tool manipulated by powers which want to hold the world in their deadly grip.

To its critics, this is further evidence that Radical Orthodoxy is sectarian, a retreat into the fortress of the Church. It speaks a language that only insiders can understand. It cuts believers off from the presence of God in the secular world and other faiths and ideologies. And it makes theology arrogant and inward looking, unable to enter into dialogue with other disciplines in the academy (the university world).

This chapter will examine what Radical Orthodoxy has to say about the nature of the Church and community in more detail. It will explore the tension – or conflict – which is set up between the Church and all other forms of human community. Particular attention will be paid to the role given to liturgy in shaping our experience of God. The highest form of liturgy, according to Radical Orthodoxy, is the Eucharist. And, as we have seen, in some of the most startling claims made by its theologians, the Eucharist is what makes all communication possible. It is the definitive model for how time and eternity interact.

We will end by exploring what Radical Orthodoxy's views imply for dialogue with other perspectives and faith traditions. Along the way, we will introduce some more critical voices and discover that the movement's own position is more complicated than it first appears.

Beginning with the Church

'The church is viewed as the social formation that renders intelligible all other formations' (*DE*, p. 262). Stephen Long's statement is a typically bold piece of Radical Orthodox rhetoric. We have already come across a number of other examples, in which it seems that Christianity alone is able to direct us to the truth. But Long's statement is different. He is not talking just about the truth of this or that doctrine. He has in mind the means by which we come up with, spell out, accept and confirm any idea of truth. The Church is not just the truth, it is the way, the only setting in which truth can be encountered and judgements made upon all other world-views.

This sort of claim may appear absurd in the context of a pluralistic society, especially one in which the Church as an institution has lost much of its prestige and influence. But, as we have seen, Radical Orthodoxy has some damning things to say about that society. And its appeal to the Church is a key part of rejecting the secular religion which has supplanted Christianity.

Long's words come in the context of a discussion of the relationship between Christian theology and economics. He asks how we make economic structures consistent with that theology, and answers as follows:

> We do not do so first by going outside the church and seeking some neutral public space in which to create a policy based on something, such as liberty, universally accessible to the human person. Instead, we begin with the church. As Stanley Hauerwas has consistently advocated, the church does not have a social ethic: it *is* a social ethic. (*DE*, p. 269)

The reference to Stanley Hauerwas reminds us of wider postliberal currents in theology. Hauerwas has been prominent in calling theology back to a proper setting within the Church. The alternative, he suggests, is that theology allows itself to be

82

dictated to by the fake universalism of liberalism. The appeal to the Church has to be understood in this context. It is a form of resistance to the oppressive powers of capital and violence. In the face of those powers, well-meaning talk about values or stories has no teeth. What is needed is a form of community which can shape people with different identity to the dominant culture. As Hauerwas writes, 'Any story that fails to provide institutional forms is powerless, for it is not enough merely to offer the story. One must know how to tell it in such a way that persons can become the story.'[1]

Radical Orthodoxy would agree. Putting the Church first ('the primacy of ecclesiology' is the phrase used by some in the movement) is not a reactionary move designed to force people into docile obedience to an authoritarian institution. It is not an attack on freedom. It is the realization of freedom, as people learn a way of being that is not defined by the dead and destructive laws of secular modernity. As Milbank puts it, 'Without "community", without its self-sustaining affirmation of objective justice, "excellence", and transcendental truth, goodness and beauty, one must remain resigned to capitalism and bureaucracy' (*WMS*, p. 282).

This community has to be the Church, because it is the Church that can embody the practice of forgiveness and reconciliation. This is something far deeper and more life-changing than the empty individualism and indifference of secular freedom:

> The universality of the Church transcends the universality of enlightenment in so far as it is not content with mere mutual toleration and non-interference with the liberties of others. It seeks in addition a work of freedom which is none other than perfect social harmony, a perfect consensus in which every natural and cultural difference finds its agreed place within the successions of space and time.   (*WMS*, p. 154)

This sounds like a tall order for any institution. But isn't it particularly hard to apply to the Church? Don't we have ample evidence from throughout the Church's history of its fallibility? Isn't the Church today divided and at odds with itself even within denominations? Talking big about the Church is one thing. How does it match up to reality?

Here is a key dilemma for Radical Orthodoxy. On the one hand, its claims about Christian truth are undermined if the Church is allowed to become just one more flawed social grouping rubbing shoulders with all the rest. On the other, if it claims perfection for the Church, it can look like it is ignoring historical reality and creating an idol. Isn't God alone perfect?

We need to understand in more depth why it is that Radical Orthodoxy should even be flirting with ideas of the Church's perfection. Several interlocking elements seem to be important here:

- Christianity is inherently social and political. It can't be turned into a private, individualistic or apolitical spirituality without abandoning the world, and so betraying it.
- The Church is about realizing the ultimately harmonious and peaceful form of community which is God's original will for creation. This fundamental calling marks it out from all other human associations.
- The Church is a continuation of the work of Christ, even an extension of the incarnation. Christ is present to us through the people who live his way and the sacraments which they share.
- If the Church accepts pluralism – the existence of many different goods – then it has effectively allowed secular scepticism and its capitalist powers to win the day.

If we take these points together, we get a sense of just what is at stake in Radical Orthodoxy's view of the Church. As we go along, however, we will also see how it deals with the less exalted reality of the Church that actually exists, and with the challenge of relating to other faiths and traditions.

The other city: the politics of the Church

John Milbank refers to Christ and the Church 'interrupting' history as the most fundamental of all events. And, he goes on to say, 'it is *most especially* a social event' (*TST*, p. 388). The social nature of Christianity is central to Radical Orthodoxy's perspective. It reflects a wider belief about the nature of being itself. In Catherine Pickstock's words, quoted earlier, 'being is that which is always already relational' (*AW*, p. 248). Reality is made up of relationships. By analogy, it shares in the nature of the trinitarian God.

The social event of the Church is therefore not one among others. It reveals the true nature of society and relationship. It shows us what creation is intended to be, and what God is like. This is why Radical Orthodoxy is so hostile to secular modernity and why Milbank's first major work was an attack on the secular social sciences. These disciplines are not neutral, scientific observations, as if we could put 'society' on the dissecting table or under the microscope and examine how it works from a detached distance. We are always already caught up in social relationships. Social sciences are no exception. They are part of academic and government institutions; they are shaped by cultural trends; they adopt contemporary philosophical assumptions. And, in the end, they produce their own vision of society, a vision which is no less ungrounded and mythical than that of any religion.

Bearing this in mind, we can appreciate why Milbank writes as follows:

> A gigantic claim to be able to read, criticize, say what is going on in other human societies, is absolutely integral to the Christian Church, which itself claims to exhibit the exemplary form of human community. For theology to surrender this claim, to allow that other discourses – 'the social sciences' – carry out yet more fundamental readings, would therefore amount to a denial of theological truth. (*TST*, p. 388)

This is a theological claim and a political claim – since, for Radical Orthodoxy, the true politics has to be founded upon theology.

This comes out very clearly in Daniel Bell's critique of liberation theology, which was discussed in the Introduction. He echoes Milbank's words, writing of 'the Church as the exemplary human community' (*LTEH*, p. 72). Remember that Bell is critical of liberation theologians for giving too much weight to the social sciences, and to their acceptance of secular models of politics. In particular, he objects to the idea that politics is 'statecraft', that it is about reforming the state with the aim of delivering a more just society.

Secular liberalism views the state in a benign light. The role of the state is to claim for itself a monopoly of violence, so that its citizens do not take the law into their own hands. This allows the state to transcend all the petty differences that might lead its citizens to fight one another. It functions as a court of last appeal, setting out the rules which order social interactions. Its code is one of liberal tolerance, as it seeks to contain reasonable differences in a neutral social space.

For Radical Orthodoxy, however, the 'state' is a modern invention devised to serve certain interests of power, national and capital. Its creed of tolerance fosters an indifference to working out the common good. It is also hypocritical, because it does not seriously challenge the inequality and exploitation of capitalism, nor does it prevent the state itself using violence against its own citizens and other states when it believes its power is threatened.

In his essay 'The City: Beyond Secular Parodies', William Cavanaugh argues that Christianity and the state tell fundamentally different stories. The Christian story is that there was a natural human unity given to us by God in creation. This harmony was shattered by disobedience, which sets us against one another. Given this sorry situation, 'redemption will take the form of restoring unity through participation in Christ's Body . . . the Body of Christ is the locus of mutual participation of God in humanity and humanity in God' (*RONT*, p. 184).

The communion enjoyed by Christians is not, however, an escape from the world. Appealing to Augustine's contrast between the earthly and heavenly cities, Cavanaugh argues that the Church interrupts 'the false politics of the earthly city'. He claims that 'It is the Church, uniting heaven and earth, which is the true "politics." The earthly city is not a true *res publica* because there can be no justice and no common weal where God is not truly worshipped' (*RONT*, p. 185).

In contrast, the state story starts with a distorted theology, in which there is no participation of humanity in God. God is commanding power, and power is necessary to bring people together. In their natural condition, according to this story, human beings are separate from, even at war with one another. They need to be disciplined and forced to co-operate. 'Intolerant' people and ideologies (like the Church) need to be tamed or excluded. The end result is not harmony and co-operation, but competition contained by law. Religion is privatized, and the Church's claim to be a community which transcends states and nations is neutralized.

Cavanaugh's book, *Torture and Eucharist*, while not part of the 'Radical Orthodoxy' series, offers an extended discussion of these themes, which runs through his argument that the Eucharist holds the key to a different understanding of human society in relation to God.[2] The main subject of the book is the Roman Catholic Church's engagement with the changing realities of politics in Chile, culminating in the brutal military dictatorship of the 1970s. To simplify greatly, Cavanaugh argues that, despite its apparent commitment to being involved in the political process, the Catholic Church adopted a view which separated politics from religion. Individual Catholics and Catholic organizations could bring Christian 'values' to bear on the state, but the Church itself had to concern itself with supernatural faith. The Church looked after the soul, the state looked after the body.

This dualism proved disastrous, however, because it surrendered the body of politics – and the bodies of those tortured and killed by the dictatorship – to a state-controlled realm in which the Church had no substantial role. Cavanaugh argues that Christianity should not separate soul and body, religion and politics in this way. The Eucharist offers a different vision, in which a different sort of community and politics can be created. This will not be a mirror image of the state, but something that goes beyond the boundaries of the state, and which binds people together through mutual belonging, not force.

It is therefore important to see that Radical Orthodoxy is not simply asserting that the Church should take over from the state, as if it were just a matter of who is in charge. To return to Bell, it is clear that he rejects the model of the Church of Constantine, when the emperor's conversion effectively made the Church an arm of the Roman Empire. He points us instead to the 'church of the poor', the Church of those on the receiving end of state-sponsored violence and economic exploitation.

Bell's argument with the liberation theologians, then, is not that they are wrong to start with the Church of the poor, nor that they are wrong to pit the Church against capitalism. Bell endorses these positions. His complaint is rather that the liberationists adopt too many of the methods and ideas of their oppressors. They shoot themselves in the foot, because secularism and the state (as conceived in modernity) are part of the problem, not the solution.

This is why Bell comes to his ultimate position, which he summarizes with what is becoming a familiar refrain:

> Christianity is the true politics, the true polity, over against the agony of capitalist discipline, in the Augustinian sense that the Church embodies the true form of human social, political and economic organization because its order is one of liturgy, of worship of the triune God. (*LTEH*, p. 4)

There are several key things to note in this passage:

- 'Christianity is the true politics, the true polity' – in other words it is both the theory and the practice of an alternative to the barbarity of capitalism.
- 'The Church embodies the true form of human social, political and economic organisation' – which means that the Church is not confined to a limited religious sphere. Its claim about how human life should be encompasses every dimension of that life. Politics and economics should not be despised as worldly and therefore impure. Nor should they be left to secular 'experts', because those experts will in fact be guided by their own (anti-Christian) ideologies.
- 'Its order is one of liturgy, of worship of the triune God' – worship is what defines the Church. The Church is liturgical, and it is worth recalling that 'liturgy' derives from Greek words meaning 'the work of the people'. Liturgy orders human work, relationships, creativity towards the divine. And God is not the mirror image of an earthly king or dictator, ruling over the universe by arbitrary decree. God is triune, the Trinity, made up of relationships of mutual love.

Bell argues that forgiveness is the key distinctive practice that the Church has to offer. Secular ideas of justice fail to break people out of the cycle of exploitation, of violence and revenge. In particular, ideas of human 'rights' have a negative impact, because they are powerless to bring reconciliation between people. When we claim our rights, when we claim justice, we want what is due to us. We want our just deserts. The problem comes when we find ourselves locked in conflict with other people, also claiming that their rights should be honoured, and that justice is on their side.

Strict justice is that of an eye for an eye and a tooth for a tooth. It leaves no room for mercy or for grace. It works within an economy of scarcity, in which a finite amount of goods have to be 'fairly' shared out. This model never overcomes conflict and competition for scarce resources.

Bell argues that Christian forgiveness can break the cycle of violence. Unlike abstract ideas of justice, it moves people into a genuinely new situation: 'Forgiveness overcomes the irreversibility of injustice precisely as an innovative movement, as the outflowing of the divine plenitude that ceaselessly gives more and gives again, graciously bearing the refusal that injustice embodies and the suffering it inflicts' (*LTEH*, p. 152). This forgiveness flows from fullness, not scarcity. Its truth is grounded only on faith that this is how God deals with sin. And this is why it must be rooted in the practice of the Church. Forgiveness is not a free-floating concept. It has a specific content and shape, defined by the way in which God forgives us in Christ.

Bell therefore claims that 'The gift of forgiveness is made available through participation in Christ, which is to say, in Christ's body, the Church. The gift of forgiveness is a communal endeavour' (*LTEH*, p. 164). Note the distinctively Radical Orthodox tone. Participation is again the key idea. Forgiveness is not a theory or an ideal, but a lived reality, lived by a community that is shaped by its worship of a forgiving God.

Bell is aware that his position faces some weighty objections. Forgiveness can sound like a convenient way of keeping the Church of the poor in its place. Effectively, the poor are being told that they shouldn't fight for their rights, they shouldn't claim justice. Like Christ, they should forgive their persecutors even as they are being crucified. Isn't this the way the rich and powerful have always used religion, to be what Marx called the 'opiate of the people', keeping them docile and resigned to their lot?

The response given by Bell is twofold. First, the Church of the poor lives out forgiveness as a witness against the dominant powers in the world. It is not merely passive. Forgiveness is proclaimed as a conversion, a break with what has gone before, a new reality. Second, the Church offers ways of reshaping people and communities to live out this forgiveness. It does this primarily through its worship. This is why it is important to note that forgiveness is not just an individual's response to wrong. It is a community's way of life, sustained by its worship which allows it to share in the forgiving reality of God, and therefore offer an alternative way of being in the world.

It is doubtful that this would satisfy Bell's critics. As we will see in the final chapter, some accuse him of a sentimentalized view of forgiveness, which aligns human suffering with the suffering of Christ. They argue that this simply gives the green light to the savage capitalism Bell wants to resist. Feminists have long known that the example of the crucified Jesus can be used to keep silent those who are being oppressed.

It is important to note for now that Bell might well be untroubled by such criticisms. He would claim to be offering a dignified alternative to capitalism, which resists the temptation to take up the weapons of oppression to fight its corner. And he would be happy to accept that the alternative offered by the Church doesn't fit with 'common sense' ideas of justice and fairness. Instead, it tries to answer to the costly, forgiving nature of how God acts.

As we saw in the introduction, Radical Orthodoxy shares the postmodern view that all knowledge has a history and a context. There is no view from nowhere. It also accepts that knowledge is socially produced, embedded in the practices of communities. This applies to the very ideas of knowledge, practice and community themselves. It follows from this, they argue, that theology has to be embedded in the Church. And the Church tells a story that takes in the whole of reality, a story which Radical Orthodoxy claims is unique.

This helps to explain why we find such extravagant things said about the Church. We have already encountered the claims that the Church is the exemplary community and the true politics. Milbank sets the standard even higher by stating that 'The Church itself, as the realized heavenly city, is the *telos* of the salvific process' (*TST*, p. 403). The *telos* is the goal, the purpose to which all things lead. Milbank is arguing that the Church is more than a means to an end. It is an end in itself.

We can see why Radical Orthodoxy believes that the Church is more than an optional extra. The fashionable modern idea that one can be a Christian without going to Church is dismissed. A certain way of being in community is the *essential* content of Christian faith. 'Believing without belonging' is just the consequence of the secular world's privatization of religion into a domestic, individual sphere which poses no threat to the way things are. Secularism can tolerate any amount of private faith and superstition. What it cannot tolerate is a community which seeks to embody an alternative to secularism in a material and social way.

Milbank writes that 'Christianity (and not even Judaism, which postpones universality to the eschaton, a final chord) uniquely has this idea of community: this is what the "Church" should be all about.' And he underlines the belief that the Church reveals God's nature: 'The community is what God is like.'[3]

These statements help to put into context the worries that Stephen Long, for example, expresses about admitting that the Church is fallible. He accepts that there is a place for protest and reform in the life of the Church, but such protest must come to an end. The Church must be reunited, because Christians must believe that the Church does not, ultimately, go astray.

It is Milbank who seems to spell out the logical consequences of this approach:

> unless the textual and ecclesial representation of Jesus – and so its relationship to Jesus, which must be a kind of 'incarnation' of the procession of the Holy Spirit – is in some sense 'perfect', how could Jesus' perfection be at all conveyed to us? (*WMS*, p. 162)

In Radical Orthodoxy's own terms, this makes sense. The Church comes first. We don't have any access to Christ (and so to a true image of God) without the Church's tradition and worship. If we assume that the Church is fallible and inadequate, this will mean that the Church can only hand on a fallible and inadequate Jesus. This will quickly be relegated to the level of one story, one image among many. If you want to be a Christian, if that's your thing, that's fine for you, says the secular world. Go ahead. Just don't expect it to affect *me* in any way.

The objections to Radical Orthodoxy's view can easily be stated. First, it idealizes the Church with little regard for its actual historical existence. The Church is often spoken about without any clear reference to anything that actually exists. And this is a serious drawback, because Radical Orthodoxy cannot be content with a merely ideal Church. The Church must embody, actually live out the forgiving practice of faith. Without this practice, without the worship to sustain it, then Christianity becomes a ghostly nonentity, a travesty of its true nature.

The irony of the arguments presented by Bell, Long and Cavanaugh is that they demonstrate how, on Radical Orthodoxy's criteria, the Church has actually messed things up pretty badly. Reading Long (himself a member of a Protestant church in the USA) it is hard to see how he can regard Protestantism as a valid form of Christianity at all, because he is so dismissive of any reforming tendency which insists that the Church might be fallible. Cavanaugh attacks the way Roman Catholic social teaching effectively prevented it from being the 'true politics' which the Church is essentially supposed to be. Milbank lays into the authoritarianism of the papacy as a flawed response to modernity.

If all these Christian traditions have got it so wrong, we have to ask how this is possible, given Radical Orthodoxy's high view of the Church. And we also have to wonder where the remedy is going to come from. If the Church comes first and is the condition for us to have access to God in Christ, what happens when the Church has fallen into error?

Milbank seems to be aware of this in his introductory comments to *The Word Made Strange*. Theology is 'tragically too important' because 'we remain uncertain as to where today to locate true Christian practice'. And this leads to an extraordinary claim:

> In his or her uncertainty as to where to find this, the theologian feels almost that the entire ecclesial task falls on his own head: in the meagre mode of reflective words he must seek to imagine what a true practical repetition would be like. Or at least he must hope that his merely theoretical continuation of the tradition will open up a space for wider transformation.   (*WMS*, p. 1)

There is in these words both disarming honesty and more than a touch of self-importance. We might ask how it is that the theologian can be so dismissive of the breadth of contemporary church life. Perhaps more important for Radical Orthodoxy, we appear to be left with a contradiction. If the Church is no longer sustaining true Christian practice, then the theologian's task ought to be impossible. Theory cut off from practice is lifeless. It can only be a misrepresentation of Christianity, not its continuation.

The second major objection to the high view of the Church we have been considering is that it is dualistic. It assumes that, as true politics must reside within the Church, outside the Church there can only be darkness. The potential for meaningful alliances with bodies outside the Church seems to be limited, if not positively discouraged. The ability to learn from non-Christian traditions seems to be ruled out from the beginning. This theology seems to deny that creation can participate in or reflect the will of God apart from the Church. This is not only theologically questionable, it puts barriers in the way of practically working with others for the common good. And, by idealizing the Church and demonizing other discourses, it insulates the Church from all external criticism and accountability.

Radical Orthodoxy sets great store by its opposition to dualism. It does not want to cut the world off from God, or divide soul and body, matter and spirit into different compartments of reality. However, by elevating the Church to near perfect, divine status, it arguably falls into the same trap. The Church – a virtual continuation of the incarnation, even an incarnation of the Holy

Spirit – has to be separated from the world, which is fallen and utterly ruined. And if the Church shows us what God is, then this means that God has to be separated from the world too.

Can Radical Orthodoxy offer a convincing account of the imperfections of the Church? And can it answer the suspicion that the Church it puts forward is divided from the world, shut in on itself, and hostile to all that is strange to it? To address these questions, we need to look again at the role played by the Eucharist in this theology of the Church, and in the whole question of how Radical Orthodoxy understands what it means to give and receive.

Gifts

Frederick Bauerschmidt's essay in *Radical Orthodoxy* offers a convenient summary of the Radical Orthodox view of the Church, and a bridge to a deeper exploration of the importance of the Eucharist (*RONT*, pp. 201–9).

Bauerschmidt is discussing the question of aesthetics, which is traditionally understood as the philosophy of art and beauty. In this essay, however, it has a wider scope: how what is infinite, transcendent and unrepresentable (the sublime) can yet be revealed in finite, worldly forms. Modernity sets up an unbridgeable gulf between the two. It is suspicious, refusing to believe that appearances can reveal the truth behind them. At the same time, it tries to use appearances to find self-evident certainty, a stable foundation for knowledge.

Postmodernism has two responses to this situation. One claims that we have to do without any notion of reality at all. We have to tear down modernity's own attempts to tell big stories about human progress and civilization. There is no final truth, no God, not even a stable self any more. The second postmodern response is the opposite. The downfall of modernity, with its dreams of certainty, frees us to tell stories again, and to look for ways in which the sublime and infinite could be revealed in worldly, historical ways.

Bauerschmidt invites Christians to take this second route. We are right to be suspicious of idols, but idols give way when Jesus

Christ is revealed as the true, incarnate image of God. The body of Christ is the key, understood in three ways: as Jesus Christ's own body, as the Church and as the Eucharist. Each of these is a sacrament, revealing the infinite God in the material world.

Echoing Milbank, Bauerschmidt argues that Jesus is a sign. Not a dead sign, but an 'effective' one, a sign that does something. Jesus actually communicates the real presence of God. This involves some nimble footwork, using the Chalcedonian creed which defined the union of the divine and human in Jesus for Christian orthodoxy. The distinction between the visible sign that is Jesus and the invisible and infinite God is maintained, but it is argued that the sign is assumed into a personal union with God the Word.

This is still very abstract, until we consider the actual story of Jesus in the Gospels. There we find that the way Jesus becomes transparent to God is by negating himself – being a slave, being misunderstood, being crucified. Even in the resurrection stories, he is misrecognized and disappears from view. But these negatives open the way for God to be revealed as present, as outpouring love from the divine fullness, even in the emptiest, most unpromising and most godless situations. Jesus can move us beyond suspicion of all appearances, and can become our master story and standard for all that is holy and right precisely because he does not claim this role on the basis of his own will to power and domination. The Christian story is about a gift that liberates us for participation, that empowers us to be creative and fully alive.

However, this gift cannot be confined to the historical time of Jesus' life. It must be 'eucharistically extended through history in the Church' (*RONT*, p. 211). This leads to a strong claim for the Church's ability to reveal – indeed to be – Christ for us. Gregory of Nyssa is quoted with approval: 'he who seeks the Church looks directly at Christ' (*RONT*, p. 212). Although the Church's union with God is not the same as Christ's, it is still a sacrament, and we can say with John Zizioulas, 'Christ Himself becomes revealed as truth not *in* a community, but *as* a community' (*RONT*, p. 212).

The Church is necessary because it makes visible the invisible reality of God through forgiveness and love of enemies. To live in 'ecclesial charity' (presumably different from any other sort) is to 'see' the Trinity and to mirror the relationships of love which are at its heart (*RONT*, p. 212). The Church is the story of Christ, offered to the world. The story is both complete and perfect, because Christ lived it perfectly, but it is also incomplete, because the world is not fully redeemed and the Church itself is sinful.

The last piece of this jigsaw is the Eucharist. The Eucharist 'makes' the Church, producing it as a community. And this depends on a very strong notion of Christ's presence in the bread and wine. Only if Christ is present in the sacrament himself can the gap between sign and reality be bridged, and our scepticism overcome. Otherwise, Christ is reduced to being a projection of our needs and desires, and the Eucharist becomes just 'one more human community' (*RONT*, p. 215).

For Bauerschmidt, 'eucharistic worship is more than simply one human language game among others . . . it is an act of divine speech through the priest acting *in persona Christi* [in the person of Christ]' (*RONT*, p. 215). However, the Church cannot just exist in its loving embrace with Christ. It is light for the world: 'The mutual hospitality of bride and spouse toward each other opens out to become coextensive with hospitality toward all who hunger or thirst or are naked or imprisoned' (*RONT*, pp. 215–16).

Bauerschmidt brings together many of the themes we have touched on so far: the critique of modernity and postmodernity, the importance of language and story, the central role of the Church. His high claims for the Church – that it directly reveals Christ – are tempered by the argument that the story offered by the Church to the world is not one of domination, but of hospitality. And there is a passing acceptance that the Church can itself be sinful.

A key element of the argument is the place given to the Eucharist. Bauerschmidt is sensitive to the criticism that he is domesticating Christ, making Christ a captive of the Church's worship. This is why he is so concerned to stress that the Eucharist is only valid if Christ's true otherness and freedom are preserved. But does this square with the idea that in the Church 'the invisible God becomes visible in a multitiude of acts of charity' (*RONT*, p. 214)? Does Bauerschmidt really take the historical contexts, compromises and divisions of the Church seriously? Where is the analysis of how the Church's collusion with sexism or imperialism, for example, has told a very different story to the one Bauerschmidt tells? What does it mean that at times when the Church supported crusades, inquisitions and witch hunts, it was celebrating the Eucharist, and teaching Christ's real presence? Was Christ's presence ineffective at those times? Radical Orthodoxy sometimes gives the impression that it only pays lip service to the Church's fallibility, because it really wants something different: for the Church and the Eucharist to be its anchor in the uncertainty of a contemporary world.

We have already noted how Catherine Pickstock argues that 'the event of transubstantiation in the Eucharist is the condition of possibility for all human meaning' (*AW*, p. xv). She offers a subtle and penetrating analysis of modern ideas of meaning and power, against which the Eucharist offers the healing of divisions between the world and God, matter and spirit. She contrasts the giving and receiving which are at the heart of the Eucharist with modernity's lust for power over us. Language can be recovered as a 'doxological gift' – that is, a gift offered and received in praise of God. The gift is one of peace (*AW*, pp. 235–6).

The idea of the gift has been an important topic of debate in some recent philosophy. Thinkers like Derrida have explored the idea of a pure gift. He has argued that a pure gift is impossible, because whenever we give, we expect something in return. It may only be gratitude. It may even only be the satisfying knowledge that we have given something away. There is always a return on our investment, so to speak, which prevents it being a true gift. The impossible, pure gift – one which is given without any return at all – remains an ideal, something by which we judge our ordinary mundane acts of giving.[4]

Radical Orthodoxy, and notably John Milbank, has questioned the idea that the true gift is pure, one way, without return. Milbank has argued that giving (and forgiving) brings us into relationship. There is always a mutual element to giving, always an exchange. And this is not a contamination of its purity. The ideal gift is not one way. It establishes community, communion, reciprocity. Derrida's one-way gift sounds too much like the idea that we should sacrifice ourselves to some higher power. But God does not want us to sacrifice ourselves, but to find ourselves in him (*BR*, pp. 44–60).

Pickstock takes up this theme in relation to the Eucharist, in which our offering and God's gift of himself meet. Because of the incarnation, she argues, 'to give to God is to be incorporated into the perpetual bestowal of gifts which takes place within the Trinity'. We only become who we are by sharing this mutuality in God. We become people who are able to give: 'giving enables us to give' (*AW*, p. 241). Through the Eucharist we are not given this or that object. We are given the gift of being able to share in God's nature, and so our true humanity is restored to us. Being is relational, made up of giving and receiving. The world is made up of gifts, not givens – not brute facts. There cannot therefore be anything outside of this giving and receiving. There is no 'moment before, beyond or without gift' (*AW*, p. 250).

One reason for dwelling upon the idea of the gift is that it helps us to understand why Radical Orthodoxy tries to hold two things together. The first of these is suggested by words like mutuality, hospitality, forgiveness, an openess to the stranger, to the other. We are not destined to be separate islands. Our humanity is restored when we establish and share peace with one another. The second element seems to be opposed to this openness. It is the belief that there can be no reality, no truth, no giving outside the Church and its Eucharist, because here and here alone is the gift of peace perfectly shared. The gift has no outside. As Pickstock says, 'To be within the gift, to give or receive at all, is to be within peaceful perfection, to reside within the Trinity' (*AW*, pp. 250–1).

This leads to some startling assertions about our humanity. Michael Hanby turns to Augustine for an account of our selfhood that can avoid the pitfalls of the modern self, which is cut off from the world and other selves and from God. In contrast, Augustine maintains that we do not define ourselves. We receive who we are through the company we keep and what we worship. And this gift of ourselves is also our own activity – we can only be ourselves when we accept the gift of ourselves from Christ. There is no contradiction between this gift and our freedom. In contrast, false community founded on false worship separates us from God and from ourselves. We become nothing, because we (and everything else) only have reality because we participate in God.

Hanby concludes from this that the human mind 'can only be an *image* of God, only manifest God in creation, insofar as it doxologically participates in God's charity through the historic ecclesia' (*RONT*, p. 115). In other words, unless we are part of the practising, worshipping Church we do not – we cannot – be said to have God's image in us. The Church has become the goal and the meaning of everything: 'Thus, the very form of creation, its means and its end, is Church' (*RONT*, p. 120). The implication is clear. Outside the Church and its worship, God cannot be known. In case we have missed the point, Hanby repeats it in his conclusion: 'Only within the doxological and confessional practices of the historic ecclesia is the alternative desire [to nihilism] possible' (*RONT*, p. 121).

An argument about the need to hold giving and receiving together has created an enclosed circle, in which all giving and receiving has to be channelled through the Church. The challenge to the privatization of religion and the separation of the Church from politics becomes the argument that only the Church can make God visible in the world, only the Church can offer true politics and economics. The Church has grown to consume all truth. In this perfect circle – compelling, but strangely stifling – there can be no true outside.

Again we have to ask whether this is true to a Christian account of creation. Is it credible to say that everyone who is not a part of the visible Church fails to manifest God's image? Presumably, if Christian practice is not up to scratch, we have to conclude that we can't see God's image in Christians either. Although Hanby sides with Augustine against the Pelagians – who believed that we are capable of being good apart from grace – it may be that Radical Orthodoxy is also guilty of offering salvation by works. Only, it seems, if we build the perfect Church can we be saved.

And again we have to ask what is meant by 'the Church'. Hanby's reference to the 'historic ecclesia' makes it sound as though he has something concrete in mind, but the phrase is left hanging in his text as an abstraction. Where is this Church? For, unless it is a definite, concrete reality, then there is no hope for any of us. But how could the supporters of Radical Orthodoxy – Anglican, Roman Catholic, Reformed – ever agree on this? Pickstock's Latin Mass is conveniently distant from any of these churches' current dominant patterns of worship. Gavin D'Costa has observed that 'This lack of grounded self-critical ecclesiological engagement is the major failing of radical orthodoxy. Its "church" is too often an invoked and reified figure, with "Eucharist" and "liturgy" often magically dispelling all ills.'[5]

If the logic of the Church is so all-consuming – and yet grounded in little that seems concrete – is there a risk that Radical Orthodoxy simply wants its own version of modern, abstract power: a theocracy, a Church governing all reality? And what would happen to its commitment to hospitality if this were the case?

Making up the Church

John Milbank rejects the idea of a Church lording it over the world. That would make the Church the pale reflection of modern states and bureaucracies: 'Better, then, that that bounds between Church and state be extremely hazy, so that a 'social' existence of many complex and interlocking powers may emerge, and forestall either a sovereign state, or a hierarchical Church' (*TST*, p. 408). Milbank has used this idea of 'complex space' to spell out in more detail the political implications of Radical Orthodoxy, and why it can't simply be equated with a domineering Church.

'Complex space' refers to a society in which there are a variety of centres and levels of power. Guilds, associations, universities, households, monastic orders – all of these and more have their own validity. Power and authority is dispersed. The appeal to complex space is an attempt to resist the aspirations of modern capitalist and state socialist nations to have effective control over all forms of human association.

This kind of complex space has been endorsed in Roman Catholic teaching. However, Milbank argues that it is given a conservative twist, and is used to endorse premodern hierarchies and inequalities, such as the dominance of men over women in households. This kind of teaching runs uncomfortably close to fascism, which used all sorts of corporations and associations to propagate its own myths, its patriarchy and racism. Milbank even suggests that the social teaching of Pope John Paul II can lead to a 'soft fascism' (*WMS*, p. 284). It endorses capitalist property rights, and calls on firms to ensure workers' welfare, but this can undermine the truly free association of workers in unions. In this way, paternalism and totalitarianism can work hand in hand.

In contrast, Milbank is committed to what he calls 'socialism by grace'. This is a socialism not rooted in Marxist atheism and faith in the inevitable march of history, but a *Christian* socialism (*BR*, p. 162). Unfortunately, because socialism was taken over by atheist forces, church teaching, and particularly Roman Catholic teaching, lurched to the right. Nevertheless, Milbank believes a Christian socialist tradition can be revived, and offer a progressive alternative to capitalism and dictatorship.

It will come as no surprise to find that this socialism is 'fundamentally liturgical' (*BR*, p. 180). It can only offer an alternative to the worship of power and acquisition that is capitalism and consumerism if it establishes an alternative relationship to the transcendent. Milbank's account of this socialism by grace is suggestive. He writes of shared festivals and liturgical public spaces. Of education free of the interference of 'democratic' politicians, and oriented to the love of wisdom. And of professions freed from endless bureaucracy, with rites of initiation and an ethos that what is produced is a gift for the community. The market would remain, but exchanges would no longer be dominated by profit and loss, overseen by guilds, co-operative banks and financial courts.

It is notoriously difficult to provide an account of such an alternative to capitalism without the details being sometimes vague and the tone sounding utopian and unrealistic. Milbank has done more than many theologians (and socialists) to give some flesh to the bones. My point in dwelling on this political vision here, however, is that this vision of socialism is Milbank's answer to his own question: 'How is the peace of the Church mediated to and established in the entire human community?' (*BR*, p. 162).

Three points are worth bringing to the fore:

- The Church does have something to offer to the whole human community. As we have seen, its vision is political to the core. For Milbank, this means that it cannot turn in on itself away from the world.
- Milbank avoids a 'theocratic' solution, in which the Church as a single centre of power dominates society. Power is dispersed. He argues that 'socialism need not retreat to a premodern contemplation of eternal positions and pre-given hierarchies' (*WMS*, p. 283). He agrees with Pope John Paul II that democracy can become a slave to propaganda, but argues that 'the antidote to this cannot merely be the entrusting of truth to a sovereign power or clerical/clericist caste' (*WMS*, p. 285).
- Milbank is also clear that the Church needs to be self-critical. The 'character of current ecclesial (and not just *Roman* Catholic) institutions' has to be held to account for its collusion with capitalism and fascist ideology (*WMS*, p. 285).

These points suggest a rather different take on the nature of the Church and its relationship to the world than the one we have been tracking so far. There is no abandonment of the need for community rooted in the transcendent and centred on liturgical celebration, but the role of the Church seems more modest, and the form of that liturgy more open to debate. The idea of the Church – like that of socialism – begins to look more like a work in progress than something complete and perfect.

The Church's role in Milbank's vision of socialism is not one of domination. *Theology and Social Theory*'s promotion of the 'haziness' of the boundary between Church and state sounds very much like Anglicanism – or, specifically, the established Church of England. The Anglican identity of Milbank, Ward and Pickstock rises to the surface in their blurring of boundaries between Church, culture and politics, while rejecting the centralized authority they see in current Roman Catholicism.

Milbank brings this out explicitly in his response to the dialogue between Radical Orthodox and Roman Catholic theologians:

> Radical Orthodoxy favours no theocracy, because theocracy is predicated upon the very dualism it rejects: for the sacred hierophants to be enthroned there must be a drained secular space for them to command. But for Radical Orthodoxy there is no such space.
>
> (*ROCE*, pp. 36–7)

God, or the Church, can't be set over against the world, controlling it from a great height. Radical Orthodoxy does not accept that there is that kind of separation between the worldly and the divine. Despite the Church of England's own errors in allowing the state too much dominance, it had nevertheless preserved an 'Anglican fuzziness' (*ROCE*, p. 36).

Does this fuzziness have any effect on the larger vision of the Church being proposed? In the previous chapter, we saw how Milbank uses the idea of *poesis* – creative making – as a key to understanding human culture and divine revelation. Revelation happens when our own attempts to create meaningful works slip free from our control and our limited intentions. At their best, the things we make (whether art, buildings, conversations, engineering works or whatever) are not merely 'objects' or commodities whose only future is to be used up, bought and sold. Their meaning is not yet fixed and complete, and their value can't be reduced to monetary terms, or to the advancement of our narrow self-interest. They are able to communicate, to bring people into relationship with one another and, crucially, with God. Our freedom and creativity is not in competition with God's. We meet God, share in God's creation, through the work of our hands and minds.

In the previous section, we raised the concern that Radical Orthodoxy might be another version of salvation by works. That remains a problem if the movement expects us to create a perfect Church in order for God to be revealed. Milbank suggests that we should see 'all true *poesis* as liturgy' (*BR*, p. x). Is this Christian imperialism – a bid by the Church to claim ownership of everything that is creative? Or is it something more open-ended? Milbank goes on to say that, alongside this creative production, there must also be exchange, relationships of mutual giving and receiving. Again, the question is whether this is confined to the Church, or whether the Church itself has to give and *receive* what it is by engaging with wider human culture. If all true *poesis* is liturgy, this might just mean that the Church isn't the only place where liturgy happens. Perhaps God's creativity is being made known elsewhere.

Responding to concerns that his view of the Church might be too overblown, Milbank denies that he sees the Church as a utopian, perfect society. The peace of Christ is already given, but not yet realized in the world. The Church therefore has a rather more fragile character than some Radical Orthodox rhetoric seems to allow. And he adds, 'Fortunately the Church is first and foremost neither a programme nor a "real" society, but instead an enacted, serious fiction.'[6]

This is a striking statement. Does it mean that Milbank has given up on any talk about the truth of the Church and its faith? Are we just making it up as we go along? Does this mean that God and reality are just human projections – the creations of our ways of speaking? Is Radical Orthodoxy actually much closer to the radical anti-realist theology of figures such as Don Cupitt, who argues that there is no objective truth out there beyond our language, and that religion should be practised purely as a human construction, a way of giving meaning and shape to our life?

We need to remember that 'truth' in Radical Orthodoxy is not a simple correspondence between our words or ideas and a reality which exists separate from us, out there on the other side of our language. Truth is a dynamic relationship: 'truth, for Christianity, is not correspondence, but rather *participation* of the beautiful in the beauty of God' (*TST*, p. 427). Milbank goes as far as to say that 'the relationship of God to the world becomes, after Christianity, a rhetorical one, and *ceases to be anything to do with "truth"*' (*TST*, p. 430). This can certainly sound close to an anti-realist position. Remember that Milbank does not believe in fixed substances. Like language, reality itself is made up of shifting differences. Out of this material, we have to construct meaning. However, the difference for Radical Orthodoxy is that when we do this, when we become creators, we find that we are also creatures. God's creativity is discovered in the things we produce, as they take on meaning and power beyond anything we could have imagined.

So 'fiction' is not the same as untruth, nor is it merely an escape from reality. It is the way we make meaning and encounter God's creative action. When Milbank says the Church is a fiction, he is drawing attention to this way in which we make and receive truth. Truth is not just correspondence, but nor is it just the projection of human ideas on to the blank screen of the world. Truth is a relationship, an event, an openness to the creative unfolding of differences. This is more than a mere language game, because Christians believe that God is Trinity, 'an absolute that is *itself* difference, inclusive of all difference' (*TST*, p. 429). God is made up of relationship, mutual love and worship. This is what secures the truth of the world. If we believed that the ultimate reality were an empty void, or an absolutely single power, then the world with all its rich variety would be ultimately worthless. We would have to embrace nihilism, or some kind of other-worldly escapism.

The important point to grasp is that Milbank's talk of fiction and rhetoric is an attempt to get us to think about truth very differently. A truth that is made up and acted out is the only truth that can connect us with the reality.

This has implications for the kind of Church Radical Orthodoxy believes in – implications which some of its own supporters have not always recognized. The God who is inclusive of difference implies a Church that is similarly inclusive. As Milbank writes: 'Revelation is not in any sense a layer added to reason . . . It is lodged in all the complex networks of human practices, and its boundaries are as messy as those of the Church itself' (*BR*, p. 122). Truth is not something imposed upon us from above, for 'Theological truth first of all abides in the body of the faithful'. Milbank develops this thought in a suggestive way:

Yet where are their plural bodies, especially today? Not neatly gathered in, that is for sure: rather, disseminated outwards in complex minglings and associations. A faith obedient to the Church is protected from solipsism precisely at the point where one recognizes that the Church always has been . . . itself the taking up and inter-mingling of many human traditions. It even consists from the outset in seeing how the diverse might cohere, and continues to enact this analogical mingling.   (*BR*, p. 122)

The essay from which these passages are taken goes on to discuss the nature of authority in the Church. Milbank rejects the slide towards 'invasive clerical control' that overtook the Church in the Middle Ages. The Catholic clergy became guardians of the controlled miracle of the Eucharist. Protestant pastors became the ones who told the faithful what the Bible said and what should be believed. On both sides, authority and truth were cut off from the body of the faithful.

Milbank sees a role for a hierarchy in the Church, but only one that is rooted in and serves the essential democracy of creation, the harmony and equality of the Trinity. Bishops have a role in preserving a tradition which can resist the anarchy and inequality of the market. But they are not mini-emperors.

Theology is accountable to the Church, but it is not to be dominated by clergy who want to preserve their vested interests: 'theology is a participation in the mind of God before it is obedience to any authority, whether scriptural or hierarchical' (*BR*, p. 133). This ideal might sound highly suspicious, a way of preserving theologians from criticism by asserting that they know the mind of God. We have already seen how Radical Orthodoxy can claim to be virtually keeping Christianity going by its own efforts.

Alongside this potential delusion of grandeur, however, there is another side to what Milbank is saying. He is arguing for a Church in which theology is free from arbitrary control, in which lay people are the ones who reveal God's truth, and in which there are many centres of power and authority. It is a vision closely related to his account of socialism in wider society.

The Church, then, cannot turn in on itself ('solipsism'), nor can it act like an army or the crowds at the Nuremberg rallies. Its boundaries are blurred and messy. It is something we make. We have already seen how Milbank admits that the key doctrines of the incarnation and atonement cannot just be read off the page of the Bible. They are innovations, speculations – they are invented.[7] The only justification for them is their attractiveness, the compelling way in which they tell the story of Jesus as God's word, and support the Christian practice of mutual love and forgiveness.

Despite some of the grand statements made by Radical Orthodox writers, this implies that the Church is something improvised and partial. God is never simply captured by its stories, beliefs and liturgies. Theology always therefore has to be tentative about where the Church actually is, who is in it, and how it is defined. 'Christianity should not draw boundaries,' says Milbank.[8]

This inclusive tone is often missed by Radical Orthodoxy's readers, understandably, given the apparently exclusive and belligerent tone of some of its claims. It is interesting to note Milbank's comments in the new preface to the second edition of *Theology and Social Theory*, issued in 2006: 'while "positively" I recommend Catholic Christianity as the one final and universal truth, I quite clearly envisage Catholicism in "liberal" terms, if by "liberal" one connotes the generous, open-ended and all-inclusive' (*TST*(2), p. xxiii).

Milbank is responding to the contradictory charges made by his critics. Some accuse him of wanting a nostalgic, conservative return to premodern Christianity. Others point to his embrace of history, which can sound like a warmed-over liberalism, which offers no sure foundation for truth beyond the ebb and flow of human cultural development. Milbank rejects both options, taking up a position between (or beyond) the two. In this latest reflection, he is more open to the welcome developments of modernity, in which language, literature and history are 'now seen as essential to the disclosing of the truth' in a way even Aquinas did not grasp (*TST*(2), p. xxix).

This leads him to restate his view of the Church. It is worth quoting this complex passage at length:

In the Incarnation, God as God was perfectly able to fulfil the worship of God which is nevertheless, as worship, only possible for the creature. This descent is repeated and perpetuated in the Eucharist which gives rise to the ecclesia, that always 'other-governed' rather than autonomous human community, which is yet the beginning of universal community as such, since it is nothing other than the lived project of universal reconciliation. Not reducible to its institutional failures and yet not to be seen as a utopia either, since the reality of reconciliation, of restored unity-in-diversity, must presuppose itself if it is to be realizable (always in some very small degree) in time and so must be always already begun. (*TST*(2), p. xxxi)

Milbank here summarizes many of the Radical Orthodox themes relevant to a discussion of the Church.

- It continues what began in the incarnation, particularly through the Eucharist.
- However, it is 'other-governed' – it must never mistake itself for God.
- It is a lived project of reconciliation, which is the beginning of universal reconciliation – it is directed towards the world.
- That reconciliation is already perfected in Christ, but not in history. So the Church is not just another flawed institution. But nor is it a utopia. It only exists through what Milbank goes on to call the 'mess' of institutional debate and conflict.

This helps to clarify why, just after the passage we quoted earlier, when Milbank seems to insist that the Church has to be perfect if it is to communicate Jesus' perfection, he admits that recognizing this truth will depend on 'a sifting from the many human "imperfections" in the ecclesial transmission process' (*WMS*, p. 162).

It is questionable whether Radical Orthodoxy has always maintained this balance. It has sometimes seemed to place too much faith in the perfection of a rather rootless, timeless and idealized Church and its sacraments. Milbank's reflections do seem to offer the possibility of other conversations. After all, he is faced by the same problem as more liberal approaches. On what grounds do we 'sift' the good from the bad in the Church? If there is no infallible authority set over it, and if its own practices and stories can be marred by conflict, doesn't this make Radical Orthodoxy's appeal to sharing in the mind of God look rather hollow? Where, for example, does Radical Orthodoxy stand on questions that divide the Western Church today, such as the authority of women and the nature of sexuality? As we will see, these issues have led some of its writers to make their own call for more practical change in the Church's life.

We might suspect nevertheless that Radical Orthodoxy's admission that the Church is imperfect is grudging. However, Milbank does want to affirm that truth is made known through the open-ended story of history, rather than simply appealing back (or up) to a static perfection.

Graham Ward also offers a much more positive reading of the Church's unstable identity. We have already seen how his reflections on the body of Christ suggested that bodies and identities are always in relation to one another. They are not self-contained wholes. This applies to the body of Christ too – to Jesus, to the Eucharist, to the Church. The Church in particular cannot claim to be the only reality, the sole community where God is known, because 'God cannot be housed'. And this leads Ward to make a statement that is bold in Radical Orthodoxy's terms: 'The institutional churches are necessary, but they are not ends in themselves; they are constantly transgressed by a community of desire, an erotic community, a spiritual activity' (*CG*, p. 180).

The institutions are necessary. Otherwise, Christianity would be reduced to a private pastime, a disembodied spirituality. However, desire – the desire for God, for one another – cannot be contained neatly within any Church. This is something to which we will return in the next chapter. For now we need to note Ward's point that the Church should be 'permeable'. As he puts it:

> The body of Christ desiring its consummation opens itself to what is outside the institutional Church; offers itself to perform in fields of activity far from chancels and cloisters. In doing this certain risks are taken and certain fears can emerge within those who represent the institution. (*CG*, p. 180)

There is something to be valued in this openness. Without it, the Church becomes another commodity, a mausoleum, a theme park. It becomes dead space (recalling Pickstock's critique of modern secularism). However, we are still left with questions. If Christianity's story is the only way of telling the truth, and if the Church is part of that truth, is it ever really capable of being self-critical and inclusive, as Ward wishes? Even his own language speaks of the Church going out, serving, 'writing God's name elsewhere in the world' (*CG*, p. 181). The idea of the permeable body might just then become another ruse for the Church to claim all truth for itself, for 'the expansion of the identified Word to embrace all that is other' (*RONT*, p. 170). Does this embrace, this inclusion, come at the price of smothering any real otherness? If the Trinity already includes all difference within itself, doesn't this devalue the freedom and dignity of creation, as a creation other than God? A Church which reflects this Trinity might, in a strange and ironic way, find itself becoming privatized after all. Listening only to its own accents, seeing nothing but its own images, recognizing no difference which it hasn't already made part of itself, the Church could become the ultimate solipsist.

So is there any sense in which the Church needs to receive from the world as well as give to it, to learn to discover God's presence and read God's name written in different places, in different languages? If language and story are not self-contained, instruments of power which can define and capture the truth in an absolute way, this implies that it is possible for Christians to enter into dialogue with people of other faith and secular traditions. Can Radical Orthodoxy accept this?

The end of dialogue?

At first sight, the answer to this question appears to be a resounding 'no'. We have already come across a number of instances where Radical Orthodox writers have said that 'only' Christianity can redeem the world, cure our sickness, see the truth. Milbank sets the tone when he writes that 'Christianity's universalist claim that incorporation into the Church is indispensable for salvation assumes that other religions and social groupings, however virtuous-seeming, were finally on the path of damnation' (*TST*, pp. 387–8). Is this what his 'inclusivity' amounts to: that Christians believe all will be saved, but only by being swallowed up by the Church?

Indeed, we have seen it suggested that those who are outside the Church have no share in the image of God. James Smith, discussing the claim that only Christianity can really be ethical, raises the question of whether non-Christians can be good at all. He is 'inclined' to the view that 'Morality or authentic virtue is possible only for the community of the redeemed . . . What appear to be instances of mercy or compassion or justice outside the body of Christ are merely semblances of virtue.'[9]

This appears to be a monstrous argument. Non-Christians cannot be good by definition, on a priori grounds. Even when evidence is produced that they are acting in virtuous ways, this is dismissed as an illusion. It is a position which is totally impervious to evidence or contradiction. It seems to rule out any meaningful co-operation or conversation with the 'unredeemed' (and who knows how it deals with the imperfection of the Church itself). The fact that it is stated in a footnote only underlines just how dismissive the sentiment is. A marginally less outrageous comment is found in Milbank's own essay 'Can Morality be Christian?', discussed earlier. He argues that outside of Christianity, all morality is reactive and in league with death and scarcity. Secularism cannot overcome death, only vainly try to hold it back. Milbank writes that 'given the death-fact, the best we can do is to be virtuous, not kill and not cause to suffer, become doctors and firemen and so forth' (*WMS*, p. 224). It is this rather petty way of writing off secular callings that makes Radical Orthodoxy sound arrogant and detached.

Milbank does, however, offer a far more interesting justification for his opposition to the idea of dialogue between religions in an essay called 'The End of Dialogue'. His argument is primarily directed at the book *The Myth of Christian Uniqueness*, a collection of essays which in different ways argued that Christians should embrace the validity of non-Christian religions and their approaches to God or ultimate reality. The argument is made up of four parts:

1   The idea that there is an abstract and general thing called 'religion' is a western invention, which cuts the huge variety of human religious practices to fit the same template. It is assumed that all religions are about the same thing directed to the same end:

> The very idea that dialogue is a passage for the delivery of truth, that it has a privileged relationship to being, assumes that many voices are coalescing around a single known object which is independent of our biographical and transbiographical processes of coming to know.   (*ED*, p. 177)

Radical Orthodoxy insists that there is no such neutral view from nowhere. The idea that dialogue partners are equal sounds welcome. But in fact, one can only assume this in advance if one also assumes that they are all on about the same thing, and usually this means that 'one takes them as liberal, Western subjects, images of oneself' (*ED*, p. 178).

Milbank argues that this approach ends up by emptying faith traditions of their content. In Christianity's case, this means that the Church is ignored, because religion is treated as a set of beliefs rather than a social project. Again, a high claim is made of the Church's uniqueness: 'no other religious community comprehends itself (in theory) as an international society' in which all are equal and committed to 'perfect mutual acceptance and co-operation' (*ED*, p. 179). The particular claims made about Jesus should not be ditched either, because they serve this universal community. It is not so much Jesus as an individual, but Jesus as a metaphor and example of perfect humanity which shapes the Church.

2   The idea that religions can be brought together on the basis of shared values and practice (putting beliefs to one side) is therefore naive. Practice and belief go together, each shaping the other. And the practices of the different faiths are as con-

tradictory as their beliefs. Where consensus exists, it is usually because people of faith have replaced their own tradition with the values of western liberalism. Dialogue is irrelevant to the poor, for example, because they do not primarily need to be 'listened' to. They need to have their poverty ended (along with the liberal consensus that keeps their poverty in place).

For Milbank, to claim the high moral ground by arguing that no religion can have a monopoly on truth leads only to a liberal western monopoly. In fact, there is nothing wrong with judging the practice of another culture to be wrong in some respect, as long as it is admitted that this judgement is made from one's own cultural reading of the world: 'if it were accepted that all cultures (religions) have equal access to the (religious) truth, then all critique, including critique' of sexist and racist constructs, would become impossible' (*ED*, p. 184).

3 Pluralism therefore cannot deliver justice. This is partly because the idea of justice related to an ultimate Good is not one shared by eastern religions, which allow conflict to continue while seeking to remain unaffected by it. So, although western ideas of justice have been used to promote imperialism, they are also the only hope for undermining that domination and violence. Justice cannot be established on the basis of 'universal human reason'. When we attempt to do this, we just set the bad version of western liberalism above criticism. And this promotes an indifferent tolerance rather than a real encounter with the Other.

4 Pluralism is not the same as trinitarian difference and harmony. Pluralism does not lead to real reconciliation. Versions of pluralism in other religions (the Hindu Vedantic tradition is discussed) are still based on conflict. They do not offer a way beyond it.

Milbank claims that eastern religions do not value the other as other. Only Christianity can do this:

> With an extreme degree of paradox, one must claim that it is only through insisting on the finality of the Christian reading

of 'what there is' that one can both fulfil respect for the other and complete and secure this otherness as pure neighbourly difference. (ED, p. 189)

In his conclusion, Milbank recommends replacing dialogue with 'mutual suspicion' and a commitment to the Church's specific project of reconciliation. He ends on another paradoxical note: 'we should indeed expect to constantly receive Christ again, from the unique spiritual responses of other cultures. But I do not pretend that this proposal means anything other than continuing the work of conversion' (*ED*, p. 190).

It is important to note that part of Milbank's objection to 'dialogue' is that it masks an essentially oppressive approach, which is unable to respect the other as genuinely other. Ironically, dialogue assumes that we are really all the same – hardly a good basis for encountering differences!

However, Milbank's own approach invites some questions. First, does he really offer a fair reading of the 'others' he discusses? Eastern religion is characterized extremely narrowly before being given a standard Radical Orthodoxy dismissal. And yet, by Milbank's own admission, there are parts of that hugely complex culture (for example, non-violence in Buddhism) which challenge its dominant view of power. If this is so, doesn't it imply that there is some valid insight and practice within Buddhism? Another example would be Milbank's insistence that only the Church claims to be an international community. Surely this is what the Muslim *umma* also claims to be? There may well be vital differences in how this is understood in the two faiths, but it cannot be ignored without distorting our view of Islam. Second, is it really necessary for dialogue to believe that people are essentially the same, or that we need to jettison our particular beliefs and practices? Can't dialogue be self-critical and critical of others? Third, if Christianity and the Church are so unique, how is it possible to receive *anything* from others? If, as Milbank seems to end up saying, Christians can find gifts in other faiths, doesn't this open up some cracks in its own absolute finality?

Graham Ward's approach to interfaith relationships can shed some light on these questions. His tone is certainly different, more modest. But is there any substantial difference between him and Milbank?

At the end of *Cities of God*, Ward notes that the 'analogical world-view' he has been putting forward is 'explicitly Christian'. However, he acknowledges that other faiths 'will construct their own analogical world-views'. They will do so differently. But analogy suggests that differences are not absolute: 'Because of the nature of analogical world-views, there can be no tight and policed boundaries around any of them . . .' There can be no call, therefore, to 'defend the walls of some medieval notion of Christendom'. As a result of this, Ward characterizes his relationship with those of other faiths in a very different manner to Milbank. He would be cautious, and insists that 'As Christians we need to suspend judgement concerning other faiths' (*CG*, p. 257).

This does not mean that Ward accepts that there is any neutral place, or any universal human essence or reason which everyone can agree upon. Each tradition has to sink more deeply into its own unique grammar. However, the results of this cannot be pre-judged: 'The real questions about the relation of different faith communities and traditions only emerge as we learn to live together without fear' (*CG*, p. 258).

There is no betrayal of the nature of the Church in this, because 'as Christians we belong to a community that is open-ended, and, therefore, continually has to risk'. There has to be 'a movement beyond the narrative which binds Christian practice and formation through a deepening sense of the rich interpretative openness of that narrative. The Christian community always waits to receive its understanding, waits to discern its form.' The Church admits to 'non-knowing' (*CG*, p. 258).

This confession that 'We do not know how the story ends and we do not know how far we have come in the plot' (*CG*, p. 259) has not found a ready welcome among all Radical Orthodoxy's supporters. James Smith criticizes the tendency in Ward to make the Church's boundaries so permeable and uncertain that it seems to coincide with all of humanity. He observes that he finds it difficult to understand why Ward remains a Christian.[10]

However, as Smith himself goes on to admit, and we have seen, these tendencies to proclaim a Church without fixed boundaries are present in Milbank's work too. The difference seems to be that Milbank believes that, for all the messiness of the Church, we still need to affirm that it practises and shares the truth in a definitive way. Part of the paradox, as we have seen, is that Milbank believes that only by stressing Christianity's exclusive truth can we create an inclusive community, truly able to respect the other in her difference.

The challenge Ward offers to this is telling, because it does not appeal to the liberalism generally despised by Radical Orthodoxy. Instead, Ward suggests that the openness and hospitality of the Church's own story and practice means that it is called to a different kind of inclusion – one that does not presume its task is to incorporate all differences. The Church, limited as well as empowered by time and culture, does not see the whole picture. Its story is all-encompassing, because it is a story of the whole of Being. But it cannot know the limits of its own story, cannot tell it all at once, nor assume that other stories might not expand it.

Radical Orthodoxy does on occasion seem to be straining at the leash of history, language and culture. Despite the value it places upon them, it wants something more immediate, something that can be grasped as a whole. The way some of its authors virtually identify the Church or the Eucharist with Christ risks abolishing the otherness of God and ignoring the Church's own failings and blind spots.

Ward suggests a different direction for theology beyond liberalism. And it is worth noting that he arrives at it through an argument which puts 'desire' at the heart of theology. The next chapter will focus on this Christian desire.

Chapter summary

- For Radical Orthodoxy, the Church comes first because we only discover and speak the truth in community, and only the

Church embodies the true form of community and politics. Believing without belonging is decisively rejected.

- The Church is not meant to be a theocracy, governing everything. Instead, it resists the violent politics of the world, as practised by the modern state.
- However, some writers do talk of the infallibility and perfection of the Church. This is what allows it to tell the story of Jesus' perfection, and stops it being dominated by any other social force.
- The Eucharist is at the heart of the Church. It creates community with God and between believers.
- The problem with this view is whether it makes the Church self-enclosed, shut away in its own perfect world.
- In response to this question, Radical Orthodoxy has advocated socialism to make its vision of community have a wider relevance. However, it has insisted that this must be a Christian socialism.
- It has also admitted that the Church is something that is made up, constructed and imperfect, and affirmed its openness and inclusivity.
- However, this openness is still restricted by its belief in the exclusive truth of the Christian story, and its suspicion of dialogue.
- Graham Ward's work offers a potential alternative within Radical Orthodoxy, offering to suspend judgement on other faiths and waiting for the real questions of how to relate to other faiths to emerge.

3

Desire: what we really want

The famous prayer of St Augustine addresses God with the words, 'You have made us for yourself and our hearts are restless until they find their rest in you.' The soul's desire for God is answered by God's desire for the soul. Rest is found when the soul dwells in God. Nothing else can satisfy.

This simple account of Christian desire may seem commonplace. For Radical Orthodoxy, however, it contains a rich resource for understanding who we are and the dynamics of our existence. For our purposes, it helps to flesh out what the movement sees as the drive and motivation for Christian living. What empowers it, guides it, gives it heart, vigour and fulfilment? And how does the desire for God affect our other desires?

As we explore these questions, we will also be drawn back into the tensions we identified in the last chapter. It became clear that there are – at the very least – some serious differences of tone and emphasis between Radical Orthodoxy's key figures. This chapter will explore whether this is partly due to different accounts of desire. If desire is always a longing for the Other, how do we understand that? Is the Other always defined in advance by the Christian story? Or is desire too fluid to be caught by such controlling definitions, flowing over the boundaries we make and meeting otherness and strangeness we did not anticipate?

We begin by looking at how Radical Orthodoxy has levelled its critical guns at the account of selfhood and desire given by modernity.

Technologies of desire

In our discussion of Daniel Bell's work in the Introduction, we saw that his account of 'savage' capitalism was uncompromisingly negative. One of the reasons for this is that Bell does not see capitalism as merely a set of ideas, institutions or market-related practices. It is also a school of desire. It teaches us what we should want and how we should want it, and so it dictates our identity in fundamental ways.

Bell refers to capitalism as a 'discipline of desire', as a collection of 'technologies that disciplines the constitutive human power, desire' (*LTEH*, p. 3). There are two things to note here. First, desire is central to what makes us human. We are not self-contained, isolated individuals. Through desire, our inmost self is related and connected to others, and our existence in time is given direction and purpose. In Christianity, it is our desire for God that defines who we are.

Second, desire is not just a given, a constant that never changes across culture and history. It is evoked, shaped and channelled in different ways. Crucially, Christianity claims that 'desire has been corrupted. Sin has distorted desire. Sin captures and bends desire in unnatural directions. It disciplines and enslaves desire' (*LTEH*, p. 2). In contrast, 'Christianity is about the healing or liberating of desire from sin' (*LTEH*, p. 3).

According to Bell, capitalism has captured desire in sinful ways. Its primary 'technology' that achieves this is the power of the state. The state first takes power away from the more local and particular forms of association that had regulated desire in premodern times. It then directs desire towards the service of the market. As producers and consumers, we are slaves of capitalism's machine, run by the state. The power of the state over us is balanced by the power of the state within us, as it shapes our unconscious wants and needs. Increasingly, our sense of self is invaded by the state, making us putty in the hands of the market. Even civil society, those agencies and organizations not directly controlled by the state, are still under its spell.

As we saw in the Introduction, Bell's charge against liberation theology is that it has uncritically taken up the idea that politics and the state go together. It has adopted ideas – like freedom, justice and human rights – which only stoke the fires of competition and conflict between individuals. And this ensures that capitalism's grip is unbroken. Capitalism thrives on organized conflict, which dissolves all other bonds of solidarity and makes us fight one another for our market share.

Christianity, for Bell, must offer a fundamentally different way of directing our desires. No less than capitalism, it offers 'technologies of desire'. Given the nature of the problem, 'Values and preferential options are insufficient' (*LTEH*, p. 87). They are powerless in the face of the political and economic forces that structure our lives. Instead, desire itself must be the battleground.

This does not mean that Christians should seek to suppress desire. That is a modern distortion of the faith. Rather, 'for much of its history, the end of Christianity was conceived in terms of the cultivation of a desire or passion for God' (*LTEH*, p. 88). To show what this means, Bell uses the example of the monastic Cistercian community, founded by Bernard of Clairvaux in the twelfth century. Bernard put desire at the heart of their account of human beings. It is not mere feeling or instinct, but 'a basic movement of the human being' (*LTEH*, p. 89). Nor is desire defined by scarcity or lack, a yearning for something not present. No: human desire is a response to the overflowing fullness of God's gift of life. It is positive, enriching and life-giving, not desperate, struggling and destructive.

The movement of desire was reshaped and healed by the communal life of the monastic order. The primary means for this was the liturgy, but it was continued through all sorts of relationships, rituals and institutions. It was not merely an inner process, but affected the monk's whole being, body, emotions, mind, spirit. Through similar practices, Bell suggests, Christians today can be weaned off capitalism, its superficiality, greed and violence. Even though monastic orders may not be the path for the vast majority of Christians, they can still gather in focused church communities, and still share in the life of liturgy and friendship.

This reshaping of desire must offer a different kind of community. If it is just a sedative, then it only serves capitalism. That is why Bell directs us to the practice of forgiveness as the Christian practice most resistant to capital's cycle of violence and competition. Forgiveness is possible for Christians who receive it first as a free gift from God's fullness, and who pattern their lives upon the forgiveness made known in Christ and communicated through liturgy and community life.

Bell's views echo those of many other writings of Radical Orthodoxy. Catherine Pickstock also sees contemporary secular society as driven by lack: 'This lack resides at the heart of a capitalist economy which organizes wants and needs amid an abundance of production, so that desire is secularized, and equated with the fear of not having one's needs satisfied' (*AW*, pp. 97–8). Reality is projected out from us as a system of dead objects, among which we search for the one thing that will satisfy our lack, end our desire. The tragic irony is that, once we attain that end, because it has no real life in it, it will only make us dead and inert objects too. Or else it will lead to a fundamental dissatisfaction which starts the whole pointless cycle off again.

In contrast, the Eucharist calls out our desire in response to God's overwhelming gift. The gift doesn't end our desire for God, but heightens and sustains it even as it satisfies it. Our desire for God *is* the gift we give back to him, the movement of our being towards him (*AW*, p. 247).

A key idea for understanding Pickstock's account of our relationship to God is repetition, which she understands in a particular way. Our ordinary idea of repetition is that the same thing happens again in the same way. There is an original event. And then there are repeats, which come after, and are copies of the original. Nothing essentially new happens with each repetition – it's the same thing over and over again.

The ordinary idea of repetition is actually a way of describing what happens in secular capitalism. Nothing really new or different happens. There are new products, programmes, technologies, ways of working. But everything is still geared to producing objects that fulfil our nameless lack. Different commodities simply represent different quantities of consumption. In the end, they can all be converted into money, the most abstract sign of sameness. Capitalism is constantly producing 'novelty' – but nothing new ever happens. Everything circulates along the same lines. There is no exit.

Against this, Pickstock sets the idea of 'non-identical' repetition, and applies this to the sacrament. In the Eucharist, the original event of the Last Supper is not the 'reality' of which subsequent Eucharists are dead copies. Rather, the event only becomes real and alive as it is repeated. The original is not complete unless it is celebrated again and again through time. And each time the Eucharist is celebrated, it is not merely a memory of something over and done in the past. It brings that event into the present as a gift, and opens up a new way of being in the future. We do not have to escape from the flow of time in order to be open to the other, the new, the transcendent. Non-identical repetition points to a way of living fully in time and language, but being able to encounter God within the world (*AW*, pp. 255–6).[1]

Part of the significance of this idea is that it suggests that our identity is not something given once and for all, but something in motion. Only as people moved by desire for a God who both transcends us and fulfils us can we be truly alive. When desire is captured and turned to dead objects, when we think we are masters of our identity, then we become slaves to death. As Stephen Long puts it:

> For our natures to be what they are called to be, this supernatural repetition [of the Eucharist] must become our natures. We have no substance that exists separate and secure from the plenitude of this inexhaustible gift. Our 'substance' is secure only in the expressive repetition of this event. (*DE*, p. 268)

For both Bell and Pickstock, the desire that has been perverted by modernity needs to be converted by our participation in the life of the Church, and especially the Eucharist. Michael Hanby's essay on desire in *Radical Orthodoxy* agrees. As we have seen, he asserts that being part of the 'historic ecclesia' is necessary for us to manifest God's image. He arrives at this point through a discussion of the self or human subject.

Hanby argues that our modern idea of the self is a distorted one. Descartes thought that one could arrive at the essential self by stripping away all that was external, all that could be doubted. The result is a lonely ego, asserting its own existence, essentially separate from others. Such a self, for all the radical philosophical doubt that went into making it, is easily slotted into liberal capitalism's structures.

Drawing on Augustine, Hanby argues that Christians see the self as a gift, but a gift that we need to make our own and live out. There is no simple or absolute boundary between our inner and outer worlds. We are intrinsically related. And, most importantly, we come to resemble what it is we worship, because what we worship is what we ultimately desire. If we worship what is separate, lifeless or domineering, then that is what we become. All desire that is not ordered through the Church is desire for nothing, a nothingness that swallows us. If we worship the Christian God, the Trinity, then we receive our life as a gift and are set free actively to live this gift with others (*RONT*, p. 121).

All of these writers share an extremely negative view of contemporary liberal capitalism together with an assurance that it is only through the practices of the Church that desire can be healed and converted to its true nature. At bottom, Radical Orthodoxy has a very positive view of desire as 'divine grace in us' (*TA*, p. 98).

However, its account of this also raises some critical questions. First, we have to ask whether its sweeping, negative judgement on modernity can be justified. Is it really that all desire in western society is simply under the heel of the worst form of amoral capitalism? We noted at the end of the last chapter that Radical Orthodoxy can slip into a position in which any evidence that seems to tell against its own story of things is not even considered. It is assumed in advance that such evidence must be false and distorted. If Christians outside the Church appear to be good, well, this must be *only* an appearance, and really they must be motivated by selfishness and greed. Similarly, Bell seems to be saying that if desire outside the Church appears to be directed towards justice or fairness or building genuine community, this must be because it is really founded on abstract, death-dealing perversions of goodness. All civil society is really a servant of the state and a slave of capitalism.

But can the movements that have built opportunities for education and health care, or the unions which have struggled for better working conditions and pay really all be dismissed as servants of evil? Are Greenpeace, Oxfam and Amnesty International simply the agents of savage capitalism? Granted that their ideas about work, nature, rights and so on need to be examined critically, and that these movements are always likely to be compromised, does this mean that they must be utterly rejected? Indeed, can all entrepreneurs and businesses be lumped together in a satanic mass?

On a more personal level, does this mean that any desire which is not explicitly linked to the Eucharist is misguided? If a non-Christian (or a liberal Christian) falls in love, or enjoys music, or has children, or loves the taste of chocolate, is this desire utterly corrupt? Granted that romantic relationships, enjoyment of the arts and food, and any number of other pleasures, can be compatible with lives of selfish greed and cruelty, does this invalidate all such desire?

This first question is intimately related to the second. Radical Orthodoxy's account of Christian desire is meant to give value to time and growth, to the reality of our material world. But it is not clear that it succeeds in doing this. We have already noted that the Eucharist can often be described in a way that floats free of history and the real political situations in which the Church has itself struggled and compromised.

Bell's example of the Cistercians is a case in point. He is aware that Bernard's writings on desire are not the only significant part of his legacy or that of the Cistercians. Bell cites questions about whether Cistercian life was really successful in redirecting desire, the continuing patriarchy of the monastic order, and Bernard's own political scheming, including his support for the violence of the Crusades. All of this is set aside, because Bell claims that his appeal to the Cistercians is merely an 'aid' to help us think about how contemporary Christian communities can reshape desire.

But this response is simply not good enough. If, as Bell says, the Cistercians are a 'concrete display of Christianity as an ensemble of technologies of desire', surely it matters whether those technologies actually work or not? If, for all the beauty and glory of Cistercian life and liturgy, we still find its leader supporting the bloody conquest of infidels and heretics, one is inclined to count this as evidence that the 'technology' is broken or inadequate. Otherwise, the appeal to the Cistercians is a sentimental and idealized one, with no bearing on actual life, and this is not what Bell wants at all.

Perhaps the problem lies in the desires of Radical Orthodoxy itself. As we argued in the last chapter, its writers often seem to want something that is immediate and sure, some way of fusing together the divine and the human, so no doubt or uncertainty remains. This is not what the stated intention is, but could it be the reality woven through the rather rootless and ideal portraits of the Eucharist and desire given in Pickstock, Bell, Hanby and Long?

The dilemma is shown in the passage from *Truth in Aquinas* we quoted earlier, in which desire is identified with 'divine grace within us'. Recalling ground we have already walked upon, Pickstock and Milbank are discussing the way in which 'the Eucharist situates us more inside language than ever', because it doesn't direct us to some pure 'spiritual' reality outside language: 'Nothing is present unless already interpreted and therefore as signified by a sign.' Even the physical action of tasting involves a kind of interpretation, a judgement as to what this action means (*TA*, p. 29).

However, this still leaves a problem. Interpretation is risky, it can always be wrong or go astray. Language and signs can be misinterpreted. The solution offered is revealing:

In the Eucharist, where the words of language 'this is my body' affirm that the absent depth tasted is here entirely present on the surface, then the physical taste of the believer itself confirms this. Whereas, normally, language makes taste to be taste, and yet throws it into doubt, here language speaks beyond doubting and taste confirms its trust, thereby helping to remove this doubt from language . . . taste is now entirely fused with the *Logos*.

(TA, pp. 97–8)

The physical sensation of consuming the bread and wine leaves no room for doubt. Language's capacity to mislead is abolished. Taste and Word are one.

It is hard to know what to make of this argument (let alone whether it gives a correct interpretation of Aquinas). It seems to undermine any sense that the Eucharist is a worldly action, because it denies from the outset any risk that the Eucharist could ever be misunderstood – even though we know this must have happened, given the Church's failings. Radical Orthodoxy wants so much to avoid dualism and to give value to this created world; and yet to achieve this it pushes its claim for the perfection of the Church and the Eucharist so far that they are taken out of this world.

This undermines the account of desire that follows. Desire – the divine grace – is generated because the Eucharist reveals a truth which 'is never exhausted, but is characterized by a promise of more to come'. But what 'more' can come, if we taste God directly in the Eucharist? The reason for repeating the Eucharist would be to achieve that perfect climax over and over again. The rest of our life would look pale and meaningless by comparison. Outside the Eucharist, all words would mislead, our desires would go astray. We would become like those nuns who reputedly ate nothing else but what they consumed when they went to Mass.

The ironies of this position should be clear. The attempt to save the world ends up by condemning the world outside a few Christian enclaves to darkness. But even within those enclaves, the desire for God is so identified with and fuelled by a desire for the immediate connection provided by the Eucharist, that it turns into a desperate parody of capitalist desire. The Eucharist becomes the object to end all objects, the ultimate commodity to satisfy our lack. It becomes an addiction.

127

If this is not the intention of Radical Orthodoxy, we have to ask whether it can produce alternative accounts of desire which avoid this dilemma.

Erotic Christianity

Looking around your average church congregation may not drive you wild with erotic desire. However, joking aside, this way of putting the matter can be a helpful way of understanding why Radical Orthodoxy seeks to rescue the erotic from the suppressed margins of Christian faith – and how this might lead us beyond the dead ends we have encountered so far.

Graham Ward argues that if Christians are to offer an alternative account of desire to the consumer lust to possess and accumulate, they have to undo the ways in which erotic desire has been given a bad name. In modernity, he argues, eros has been practically identified with a very narrow idea of sex and sexuality. Ward wants to rediscover a much richer vision of eros as part of his argument that 'desire is fundamental to our nature as human beings as God created us' (*CG*, p. 76).

Ward echoes the critique of secular desire made by Pickstock. It is based on lack, it will never be satisfied. 'In its very crudest form – desire for sexual gratification – however many orgasms I have I'll always want more' (*CG*, p. 76). In contrast, God's love for us does not satisfy any 'need' or lack, and, ultimately, our love for God is about sharing and enjoying the divine life of the Trinity:

> Christian desire moves beyond the fulfilment of its own needs; Christian desire is always excessive, generous beyond what is asked. It is a desire not to consume the other, but to let the other be in the perfection they are called to grow into.   (*CG*, p. 77)

The point of true desire, then, is not to possess and consume the other. But nor is it to suppress and deny all embodied pleasure. Ward recognizes that Christian theology has been guilty of an unhelpful dualism (*CG*, p. 183). Anders Nygren's famous book *Agape and Eros* was influential in the way it erected a gulf between two types of love. Eros is essentially selfish, an extension of self-love. It has to be controlled through marriage or celibacy. Divine love – agape – is selfless and pure. The implication is that eros – associated with the body, sex and our life in time with others – is too dirty to approach God. This dualism leaves our worldly desires eternally unredeemed and separate from God, hardly an adequate position for a faith that puts the incarnation of God at the centre of its life.

Christian desire does not consume the other. It respects difference. However, it does not turn this difference into indifference – a relationship without passion or the desire for intimacy, connection and mutual enjoyment. This is why Ward calls the Church an 'erotic community'. In the Eucharist, desire is not closed and grasping, trying to fix its object. It is always excessive. God is not wholly other, but related to us by overflowing desire. Our self-love is opened out to love of others. But this love is not something bloodless and abstract: 'The Christian as a subject of desire is attracted by that which is encountered. He or she responds in that attraction, which always has an embodied specificity. Christians desire this and that, him or her' (*CG*, pp. 172–3). The world therefore does not lose its richness and meaning. We do not have to sacrifice our particular loves and pleasures to a ghostly spiritual end.

Set against this vision, the kind of erotic stimulation that is constantly promoted in popular culture looks pallid, shallow and unsatisfying. To illustrate his point, Ward even indulges in a trip to a sex shop (not the usual kind of field research for a theologian). Behind the dark frontage, the sex shop is laid out for the dominating male gaze. Bodies are displayed, frozen and available. Desire is fabricated: 'All is virtual. The material provokes desire, but it can neither maintain nor fulfil what it appears to promise . . . The Sex Shop produces nothing. It exists for the endless provocation of the desire to consume' (*CG*, p. 120). As such, the shop only reveals in stark terms the reality underlying all of our consumerist society.

The erotic community of the Church offers something very different. However, the flow of desire also works to loosen the boundaries of the Church itself. We have already noted that, for Ward, the Church is never self-contained. The institutional churches are means to an end. They 'are constantly transgressed by a community of desire, an erotic community, a spiritual activity' (*CG*, p. 180).

This openness of the Church to a desire which carries it beyond its own defined boundaries is the basis upon which Ward embarks on some new territory. Radical Orthodoxy does not hold back from biting criticism of modern theology. Usually, however, it is far more muted in its reservations about what went before. Bell and Hanby recognize that there are deficiencies in Bernard and Augustine's writings and example, but they tend to play these down or reinterpret them more sympathetically. The impression given is one of an uncritical elevation of the premodern Church to ideal status. It is therefore hard to see what the concrete consequences of Radical Orthodoxy's approach are for the contemporary Church (adoption of the Latin Mass?).

Ward is also heavily influenced by the theological fathers of the Church, especially Augustine, but he acknowledges that his interpretation of Augustine is constructed. It cannot claim any absolute status. It is 'holographic', with only a tenuous relationship to the historical figure (*CG*, p. 24). This reflects Ward's view that meaning is something that we *make*. It is always mediated, filtered through culture.

Ward applies this insight to his substantial discussion of sexuality and gender. 'Queer' theorists such as Judith Butler have argued that gender is not something natural, unchanging and essential, but a socially constructed role that we perform. Ward claims that Christianity should be sympathetic to this view, because it too sees bodies and identities as unstable. In the light of revelation, we should not accept given gender roles or ideas about sexual attraction without question. What is promoted as 'natural' might well have been produced in history, in order to serve various interests of power.

The idea that all sexual desire must be heterosexual should be challenged, he argues. For one thing, it tends to fix the identities of men and women, characterizing women as dependent and passive. For another, it excludes as unnatural all same-sex relationships, even though they can reveal something of the mystery of love for the other person which goes beyond the merely 'bio-logical' or preconceived ideas about what is 'natural'. Ironically, a fixation on heterosexuality as the norm can end up obliterating real differences, forcing men and women into fixed roles where power is exercised in a one-way direction.

Ward concludes:

> The Church must sanctify difference, must examine and discern difference in all the relationships it sanctifies. For it is from difference that the Church receives the power to be and participates in the power to become. The Church must sanctify, then, genuine sexual difference through its liturgies – whether that sexual difference is evident between two women, two men, or a man and a woman. (*CG*, p. 202)

This questioning of received gender roles is also present in Gerard Loughlin's contribution to *Radical Orthodoxy*. In a complex essay, Loughlin takes the Catholic theologian Hans Urs von Balthasar as one of his major conversation partners. Balthasar affirms the erotic dimension of our relationship to God, the pleasure and passion of faith. Spirit and body, individual and community, man and woman are caught up in this relationship. The difference between these realities is not denied, but that difference is held together in unity.

However, Loughlin questions whether this ideal of erotic unity in difference is really achieved, because Balthasar still wants to give priority to one pole of the relationship. In particular, man takes priority over woman. It is the male principle which is active, the female which is passive. God must therefore become man, not woman. Loughlin suggests that this imposes upon God our conventional ideas of male supremacy, whereas the giving and receiving in the Trinity transcends these ideas. Citing Graham Ward's work, Loughlin argues:

> what our culture may dictate as our sex and gender will no longer be determinative of our freedom to give and receive love. For truly in Christ there is no male and female, only the reciprocation of bodies; beautiful parodies of the Trinitarian donation. In this way we may also discover that Mary not only has a womb, but . . . a uterus and a clitoris also. (*RONT*, p. 158)

The divine gift (donation) takes away as much as it offers. It takes away our settled certainties about what we desire and how desire works. In particular it calls into question our patriarchal assumptions that the male comes first, and is 'naturally' closer to the divine. It is noteworthy that Loughlin uses the term 'parody' instead of analogy to describe the likeness and unlikeness between God and creation. As justification for this, he says he does not want to imply that these links are not serious, but to 'disturb the ease' with which we compare God with human ways of understanding bodies, identities and desire (*RONT*, p. 144).

Ward and Loughlin are sensitive to the way that desire and sexuality are 'made' by culture. At the same time, desire resists being captured in this way, and can shake up and disturb our settled ideas. As Ward puts it, 'Desire is complex, multi-focused and held to be maintained by a power that is greater than that of any individual or even collective' (*CTRP*, p. 153). Not even the Church or its tradition can adequately tell the story of God's desire for us and our response.

In this context, it is interesting to see how this new movement, with its claims to orthodoxy, has made connections with 'queer' theory and theology, which seems to be much less compatible with traditional Christianity. 'Queer' is a term of abuse directed against all those whose sexualities do not fit the heterosexual norm. It has been reclaimed by those who want to use theory to subvert that norm, to undermine the idea that heterosexuality is natural and given.

As we saw, Ward quotes the work of the seminal queer theorist Judith Butler, who argues that gender is something constructed by society, something we *do*. However, the influence has worked the other way round too. Elizabeth Stuart has been a prominent voice in gay and lesbian theology for some years. She has argued, in common with much feminism, that theology needs to be based upon the experiences of those excluded by the Church and society – experiences which can be the basis for new, liberating perspectives on justice, love and friendship.

In her book *Gay and Lesbian Theologies*, Stuart takes a very different direction, however. She surveys the development of these

theologies, with their appeal to 'experience', and finds them wanting. The problem is that we can't just appeal to 'experience' as
something given, as a new foundation for theology. The question will always come back, 'Whose experience?' For instance,
early feminists found themselves being criticized by black writers,
because their theory was based primarily on the experience of white,
middle-class women. In response, womanism was developed, as a
specifically black feminist approach, which took the experience of
racism much more seriously.

However, this is not the end of the matter. For one thing, the
appeal to experience fragments people more and more, rather
than binding them in solidarity. After all, not all black women's
experience of racism is the same – differences of class, generation,
culture, geography and so on all play their part. And this leads to
another point: experience itself is something that is socially mediated, even socially constructed. The kinds of experience we have
and the range of experiences available to us will be shaped by our
language and our cultural context. We are not born in the world
as empty vessels, waiting to be filled up by experience. We are social-
ized, brought up, educated, influenced, so that we come to every
experience full of preconceptions, even if they are unconscious ones.
Interpretation comes first. There is no 'pure' experience.

Stuart therefore rejects the way that gay and lesbian theologians
in the past had a very uncritical idea of experience, together with
fixed concepts of gender and sexual identity. They were too much
under the spell of modernity. The result was that they lost contact with the traditions of Christianity itself. In particular, they lost
any sense of the transcendence of God, because it was assumed
that this could only be oppressive and life-denying.

Stuart therefore embraces queer theory, with its much more critical approach to sexual identity. However, she also calls gays and
lesbians back to orthodox Christianity and to the Church and its
sacraments. She cites Radical Orthodoxy, and Ward in particular,
as evidence that Christian tradition, while it might need rethinking at points, is compatible with queer theory's approach. Indeed,
she argues that queer theory needs Christian orthodoxy to save it
from hopeless relativism:

> For there is only one community charged with being queer and that is the Church, and it is so charged for a purpose: the preparation of the kingdom of heaven. Only Christianity can make queer theory a viable strategy for only Christians are called to imitate their God in acting *para phusin*, in excess of nature.[2]

Stuart is claiming that Christianity is queer by its very nature. Because it believes in a God who is transcendent, it is not bound by the social conventions of culture. It creates a new kind of culture and community, which is entered by baptism, not biology. In the end, all our cultural identities are secondary to our identity as children of God: 'Christians are then called to live out their culturally negotiated identities in such a way as to expose their non-ultimacy, to take them up into the processes of redemption. They do this by parodying them.'[3] Like Loughlin, Stuart does not mean by this that Christians do not take culture seriously. But they do seek to expose culture to 'the other world breaking in',[4] as the Eucharist exposes us to the otherness of God and to the strangeness of our neighbours. These others can't be caught by our definitions. We need to give and receive an outrageous hospitality. In the end, what matters is not sexuality, but the Kingdom of God, of which we have a foretaste in the Church.

Stuart does not necessarily see herself as part of Radical Orthodoxy, but her views show a striking similarity to the way that movement has been articulated by Ward and Loughlin. Is this an indication of how it will develop? To approach that question, we need to consider whether there are alternative trajectories within the movement – as well as hearing the critical voices which challenge its view of sexuality from the outside.

Boundary crossings

It is far from clear that all the contributors to the Radical Orthodoxy volume and series would be prepared to accept the kind of revision of the Church's understanding of sexuality and marriage outlined by Ward and Loughlin. Stephen Long, for example, in writings outside of the series, has upheld a more traditional opposition to same-sex unions.[5] Other scholars have wondered whether the kind of views expressed by Ward are much more 'radical' than they are 'orthodox'. What are the limits to his poetic speculations upon the body of Jesus, if that body exceeds all limits?

However, it would be too simplistic to divide Radical Orthodoxy into 'liberal/progressive' and 'traditionalist/conservative' camps, or to dismiss writers like Ward as simply beyond the pale of the movement. Ward's views are most clearly articulated in volumes published within the 'Radical Orthodoxy' series. And he clearly appeals to a reading of tradition in challenging fixed views of desire, bodies and genders. He would surely agree with Elizabeth Stuart that traditional Christianity has done a great deal to foster 'queer' parodies. In its liturgy, its resurrection hope, its varied ascetic and monastic practices, it has imagined possibilities for human living and fulfilment beyond given gender roles.

The question for Radical Orthodoxy is: how fluid is that tradition? It is worth noting that the suspicion of liberal postmodernism has even fallen upon John Milbank, because he has embraced the view that there are no fixed substances as entirely in keeping with – indeed, demanded by – Christian teaching. But the question still remains: how far can the desire for God and for connection with others push that teaching and tradition beyond what many Christians still see as non-negotiable boundaries? What is left of 'orthodoxy' in this situation? John Milbank's response to this question is suggested by the essay which brings *Being Reconciled* to a close: 'Culture: The Gospel of Affinity'.

He begins by asking 'what is postmodernity? Not postmodernism as a set of theories, but postmodernity, as a set of cultural practices.' Milbank answers that 'Above all it means the obliteration of boundaries, the confusion of categories' (*BR*, p. 187). He then spells this out in more detail, putting forward four ways in which postmodern culture makes things melt together:

1 The distinction between nature and culture is blurred. What was once seen as natural and fixed is now seen to be shaped or even produced by human action. Nature is never pure, it is always interpreted by us. Matter becomes more ethereal, nature (think of DNA) is made up of codes and information, while

our mental and spiritual life becomes more embodied. And there is less need to identify any stable human essence, or stable genders.

2 The inner and the outer are confused. The private self, the domestic realm, the inner sanctum, are all invaded by the public world, the media and the market. People's selves are on virtual display through blogs and websites and cyber communities.

3 Economic categories are dissolved into one another. Information now becomes the driving force of economies, more than any actual production. Service industries are now dominant. Traditional patterns of production and labour are deregulated.

4 The postmodern world is globalized. The economic realm and the political realm are united at an international level. This is accompanied by the growth of a new global, postmodern empire: 'an empire of endlessly expanding frontiers, an empire of inclusion, not remote control, and an empire able to distribute power to its peripheries' (*BR*, p. 192).

Each of these characteristics of postmodernity can be and has been welcomed as the advent of a new era of freedom, when humanity is no longer held back by false ideas about natural limits, or by the tribalism of nation states and defined identities. However, Milbank identifies a questionable thread holding them all together: immanence.

Immanence is the opposing pole to transcendence. Postmodernity – like modernity before it, but in ever more radical ways – is 'relentlessly secular' (*BR*, p. 193). All the differences and freedoms it sets in motion circle round and round monotonously. The new empire of postmodernity is a triumph of capital. Boundaries are crossed not for some noble idealistic cause, but to expand the reach of the market, to colonize every part of life under the deadening glare of stockmarket displays. Desire is endlessly recycled. It leads nowhere. There is no transcendence which would give meaning and purpose to the whole.

However, Milbank does not simply reject postmodernity and call Christians back to a premodern form of faith. He claims that postmodernity is 'a kind of distorted outcome of energies first unleashed by the Church' and explains that 'Postmodernism, I have said, is the obliteration of boundaries. And Christianity is the religion of the obliteration of boundaries.' This means that 'neither a reiteration of Christian orthodoxy in identically repeated handed-down formulas, nor a liberal adaptation to postmodern assumptions will serve as well' (*BR*, p. 196).

Neither liberal nor conservative responses will do, then. But what does Milbank mean by Christianity's obliteration of boundaries? And how does the Christianity he advocates differ from the post-modernity he criticizes?

Two points need to be held together, Milbank argues:

- In one sense, Christianity does lead us to imagine the possibility of living beyond the Law, to live by grace rather than being bound by what is 'naturally' given. It did

    > explode all limits: between nations, between races, between the sexes, between the household and the city, between ritual purity and impurity, between work and leisure, between days of the week, between sign and reality . . . above all, with the doctrine of the Incarnation, Christianity violates the boundary between created and creator, immanence and transcendence, humanity and God.   (*BR*, pp. 196–7)

- However, it is too simplistic to say that Christianity abolished the Law and all boundaries. It did not just reject its Jewish roots. The Old Testament was retained, and St Paul affirmed that God's covenant with Israel held firm. And Judaism does not obliterate boundaries. Israel is a real people, who occupy real, geographical space. For life to flourish, limits have to be set, if chaos and brutality are not to gain the upper hand.

The second point is relevant to the negative aspects of our globalized postmodern world. A world that recognizes no limit can simply be the excuse to export the oppression of labour, invade states to secure their resources, exploit nature without constraint, descend into addiction and lose any capacity to resist. Destruction and misery are the result of this illusion of freedom.

This is why Christianity's response to postmodernity needs to be complex. For example, it cannot just appeal to 'nature' to oppose practices such as genetic engineering or cosmetic surgery. Human beings, as we have seen, are created to be creators themselves, to share in the divine creativity. It is through our making, our interventions in the world, that we find God's nature revealed back to us. However, this does not mean that 'anything goes'. Instead, Christians are called to discernment. The truly made must imitate the true, must be in harmony with the way things are called to be (*BR*, p. 106). Genetic engineering or cosmetic surgery can be used to enhance the beauty of life, to make our sense of who we are richer, to open ourselves out to a greater calling. Or they can be used to turn crops, animals, babies and our own bodies into commodities, standardized 'things' which we control, with no depth to sustain them.

Christians should not simply set nature and culture in opposition, but ask how our culture helps to reveal our created nature – how the gospel shows us the inner dynamic of the Law. So Milbank is searching for a way of talking about nature and identity without falling back into the idea that these things are simply timeless givens, but gifts which we receive in and through our own creative action. As he puts it, 'there is a true way for things to be and a way things eternally are' (*BR*, p. 106).

Milbank uses the idea of 'affinity' to clarify what this means. Affinity is the mutual attraction that exists between things or people that belong together. It is a relationship, rather than an abstract substance. But it does imply that there is some structure to the world, a way in which things naturally belong together that enhances the life and being of each one. Christians claim that we have this affinity with God, that we are made in God's image. God's image in us is not just one human property (like our reason or soul), but the way we imitate and share in the nature of God, the way we come to be 'at home' with God (*BR*, p. 203).

Milbank uses this idea to outline his own approach to sexuality and gender. He argues that for much of their history, Christians have failed to realize that this affinity between God and humanity 'puts the erotic at the heart of *agape*'. The attraction between ourselves and God – and by analogy, our attraction to one another – is not an impersonal one, but 'the arriving gift of something that we must partially discover in patient quest, active shaping and faithful pursuing' (*BR*, p. 204). Our particular loves, linked by the wider community of the Church, can be a picture of the genuine peace and reconciliation of the Kingdom.

This 'aesthetic' dimension of affinity explains Milbank's otherwise surprising statement that 'we are totally wrong to approach contemporary sexual issues as primarily a moral matter, or of what should and should not be done' (*BR*, p. 205). These relationships are what make morality possible in the first place. They are not first and foremost about rules and principles, but life.

Milbank is scathing about the hypocrisy of both liberals and conservatives in sexual issues. Liberals play down faithfulness and security, but these are necessary for affinity to resist the corrosive spread of market values into every part of life. Conservatives uphold rules like 'no sex outside marriage' (for which Milbank sees 'no real warrant'), but in practice they accept that life is messier than their publicly confessed principles allow, and when faced with the realities of divorce, cohabitation and so on within their own family they are more tolerant than their overt theology would suggest (*BR*, p. 205).

As part of this attempt to put affinity at the heart of the gospel, Milbank argues that sexual difference cannot be completely dissolved away. Men and women do have distinctive biological and bodily structures, which affect how they experience the world. The difficulty is in spelling out what this means. Milbank certainly wants to avoid the sexism which identifies men with control and independence, and women with submission and passivity. However, he does state that some generalizations can be made: 'men are more nomadic, direct, abstractive and forceful, women are more settled, subtle, particularizing and beautiful – though both sexes are equally innovative, legislative, commanding and conservative within these different modes' (*BR*, p. 207).

Despite his intentions, we have to ask whether Milbank's desire to have some structure to human identity betrays him into the hands of a traditional sexist stereotype. Pitting abstraction against what is settled and particular can sound unnervingly like the old patriarchal idea that men represent reason, while women are tied to the passions and the body.

Milbank's position also leads to an odd compromise about same-sex relationships. Sexual difference seems to be necessary to resist the indifferent narcissism of postmodernity. This might seem to leave little room for non-heterosexual unions. However, Milbank writes that 'There need be no problem whatsoever with the idea that homosexual practice is part of the richness of God's Creation (nor with co-habiting gay clergy)' (*BR*, p. 207), because we are not all tightly defined by a collective essence. Milbank also offers the view that such relationships can point us towards the life of angels who have no gender.

Homosexual unions are therefore not the same as marriage, in which sexual difference is central. However, Milbank argues that there should be some sacramental celebration of such unions, which should 'be seen (beyond the received tradition) as equal in cosmic significance to those of marriage' (*BR*, p. 208).

The spirit of Radical Orthodoxy

'Equal but different' can be a smokescreen for maintaining old inequalities. Does Milbank escape this trap? He is certainly explicit in his desire to go 'beyond' tradition. His specific endorsement of cohabiting gay clergy is refreshingly direct for so dense a writer! A much more difficult passage to interpret comes when he is suggesting how sexual difference is at the heart of the Church's identity. One image he looks at is that of the Church as the bride of Christ. He proposes that 'gender equality within difference requires us, beyond the limitations of Catholic tradition, now to see the Bride as enhypostasized by the descent of the Spirit (in her full eschatological plenitude of commencement and ending) and so as equal to the Bridegroom' (*BR*, p. 208).

Several ideas need teasing out here:

- Catholic tradition is limited. Although Milbank is taking up an image from the Bible and tradition, he does not pretend that this image has in the past been used to promote gender equality.

- The Church (the Bride) is united to God by the Holy Spirit. The word used – enhypostasized – implies that this is equivalent to the way the divine Word takes flesh in Jesus. As we have already seen, Milbank is prepared to argue that the Church is an incarnation of God's Spirit.
- The Spirit brings creation into existence, and leads it to all truth and fulfilment. She is the beginning and end of all things.
- As the Spirit and the Word are equal in the Trinity, so the Church and Christ are equally embodiments of God in the world.

This is indeed a radical interpretation of – some might say a departure from – orthodoxy. But it is consistent with the themes we have been exploring throughout this book.

Radical Orthodoxy says that the truth is not available to us apart from story and tradition, and from the complex ways human beings interact with and shape our world. At the same time, it puts its faith into the particular story of Christ as the Word made flesh, who founds a new community of forgiveness and reconciliation. Only this story and this community can reach beyond our narrow tribal identities and make peace a reality. This means that the Church has to be given an exalted status, culminating in the idea that it is the Church which extends the incarnation of God.

However, here an interesting breach opens up. Milbank argues that the Church is the incarnation of the Spirit, not of the Word. Of course, in the Trinity, there is no suggestion that the Spirit and the Son or Word are in any kind of disharmony or disagreement. Nevertheless, from our perspective, we only have an imperfect understanding of how the Word and the Spirit are related. A gap can open up in which we tell different stories about them, with different emphases.

Christ broke down boundaries, but as the founder of the Church, he can be swallowed up in an institution whose main aim is to conserve itself. The Spirit seems to be a less controllable reality. The Spirit is like the wind, escaping our gaze and capture in definition (John 3.8). Perhaps it is this identification of the Church with the Spirit that allows Milbank to admit with confidence that the Church's tradition is limited, and needs to be renewed and changed in some cases.

Milbank writes of the Church as a fiction which 'invents' its doctrines. Other Radical Orthodox writers have their own ways of opening the Church and its tradition to what it cannot control. Loughlin highlights the role of parody, making us less confident that we have got the relationship between God and the world all mapped out. Ward uses the idea of the body of Christ to show that the Church is inherently open and in flux, that it must risk going beyond its boundaries, and even suspend judgement on other faiths. In each case, it is by reflecting upon the nature of desire that the theologian loosens up rigid structures.

This openness is demanded by Radical Orthodoxy's commitment to the Church as a universal community, a foretaste of the Kingdom. Given the actual churches' chequered past, this commitment can only be secured if Christians are open to discovering new dimensions of revelation.

This is, as Ward says, a risky venture. And Radical Orthodoxy can also place limits on openness. Sometimes, as with Milbank's idea of affinity, these limits can be dynamic and flexible, whose aim is to prevent desire from becoming just an abstract lust for possession and power. However, the movement can also fall into its own version of that desire – for the immediate grasp of God, contained within the historic Church.

In an essay on the Holy Spirit in *The Word Made Strange*, Milbank's understanding of the relationship between the Spirit and the Bride tends in this direction. He first makes the familiar point that Christ's atonement makes possible a human practice of atonement. He then adds that the other side to this is that 'Christ *depends* upon this [human] process'. Without the response of the Church, Christ has no effect on the world. But because only God can make the perfect response, this means that the Church must be identified with God; 'the Spirit has her own form of *kenosis* [self-emptying] in the church' (*WMS*, p. 186).

The Church is the incarnation of the Spirit. But the implication here is not one of openness, but of closure. The Church is 'the entire, true, historical response to Christ'. It is held between the objective, given reality of Christ and the subjective response of humanity in the Spirit. But it is entire unto itself, a seamless garment, whose story is 'a perpetuation of the Incarnation' (*WMS*, p. 186).

In this closed, domestic scene between the Bride and Groom, is there any space for real otherness? Does the Bride have any reality of her own? Or is she just the settled reflection of a God who continues to be male, controlling his household and keeping his womenfolk indoors? Is there any risk involved here? Or is the Church so identified with the divine Spirit, that its interpretation of the Word is always faultless?

Again, Graham Ward seems to offer a more questioning approach. Belief is always particular and constructed, so there is no God's-eye view of reality (*CTRP*, p. 87). Desire is always plural. Christian desire is 'polysemous' – rich with a diversity of meanings, and open to otherness (*CTRP*, p. 152). And this implies that the Spirit cannot be wholly contained within one single story, tradition or institution. Discussing the 'fruits of the Spirit' listed by Paul (Galatians 5.22–25), Ward comments: 'These are available not only in Christianity, which is obviously the context for Paul's admonition. They are available in the practices of other faiths. They are also available in certain other standpoints' (*CTRP*, p. 155).

There is an uneasy compromise at work here. After all, if there is no God's-eye view, how can Ward claim that the Spirit is at work in other traditions? Only, it seems, from within a Christian standpoint. And Christianity still claims that it is the Spirit of *Christ* that is at work. All knowing and desiring have to be perfected in Christ: 'relation can only be realised in the extent to which it participates in the love of Christ. The social is and can be social only insofar as it is constituted *in Christo* . . . From the Christian standpoint, there is no other body' (*CTRP*, p. 170).

Clearly, if we accept the rejection of modernity's search for self-evident certainty and absolute foundations, any claim we make for truth will be partial and contextual. Our arguments will have to be circular, because we will have to make certain assumptions about what is true in order to say anything at all. The question Radical Orthodoxy raises is: can this circle be open and hospitable? Or must it be vicious, suppressing all other points of view?

Broken beauty

Radical Orthodoxy is clear that the body of Christ exists in history. Forgiveness is only possible in the passing of time, 'and so only in passing is the Church the community of reconciliation' (*BR*, p. 105). The Church consists of signs of peace: 'Each sign is inadequate, and must make way for further inadequacies: yet in their passing, the signs compose a figure of broken beauty and of spasmodically peaceful co-existence' (*BR*, p. 106).

At several points we have noted the 'aesthetic' dimension of Radical Orthodoxy. It rejects the idea that there is a universal abstract reason or law which can determine what is true. Its recommendation of Christianity does not have such secure foundations. It is groundless.

This is why Milbank writes that there is no way of justifying key Christian doctrines apart from 'the inherent attractiveness of the picture of God thence provided' (*TST*, p. 384). Similarly, 'At the extreme limit of its possibility ethics is only a subsphere of aesthetics, governed by criteria of good taste' (*TST*, p. 357). Such statements seem to take theology and ethics out of any engagement with reason at all. They appeal to a wordless intuition of beauty.

The problem here has already been identified by Radical Orthodoxy itself: all our experiences, intuitions and judgements are conditioned by our context and by language. What counts as good taste and attractiveness differ in different settings and discourses. They are not timeless and neutral.

When Radical Orthodox writers ignore this, they are prone to use this aesthetic intuition as a new kind of foundation for asserting an exclusive truth. Among other examples we have already quoted along the way, we recall Blond's claim that only Christian theology can 'see' truly, and Bauerschmidt's line that to look at the Church is to see Christ directly. And Laurence Hemming writes that '"ethics" apart from redemption is always revealed to be in consequence of the will to power' (*RONT*, p. 105). How can we know this? We just do. There is no foundation. We *see* it.

The value of this approach is that it can free us from narrow ideas of truth and reason. As the Romantic movement sought to counter the dry rationalism of the Enlightenment by using artistic creativity to unite the human and the divine, so Radical Orthodoxy seeks a harmony that cannot be reduced to laws and logic.[6] If our desire is not oriented to the transcendent and beautiful, then we will be impoverished and at the mercy of those who manipulate desire for worldly ends.

However, we have also pointed out the potential shortcomings of this position. It can end up by claiming ownership of the transcendent and beautiful, making it the sole possession of the Church (or the theologian). And this looks uncomfortably like the way Radical Orthodoxy claims that desire is controlled and domesticated by secular powers and by the market. The circle can become vicious.

Milbank and Pickstock's discussion of desire, Eucharist and Church underlines these concerns. They argue that desire

> has to be desire for God, for only if God is real can we trust that a desire for further knowledge will be fulfilled and that signs are not empty. However, the question of desire for God should not be taken merely in an individualistic way, but rather in collective and historical fashion. (*TA*, p. 108)

The Church becomes the sole context in which signs can be trusted:

> these words and events only occur in the Church . . . The Eucharist both occurs within the Church and gives rise to the Church in a circular fashion. In consequence, the Eucharistic event inevitably involves trusting also the past and the future of the Church. (*TA*, p. 110)

The Church then can dictate when and how God is made available, and what form desire should take. The line between 'trust' and submission to arbitrary authority is a fine one.

Perhaps the idea of 'broken beauty' can provide an alternative path forward for Radical Orthodoxy. It is certainly acknowledged by various of its writers that Jesus on the cross is a strange and disfigured image, not one that conforms to accepted ideas of good taste and loveliness: 'he had no form or majesty that we should look at him, nothing in his appearance that we should desire him' (Isaiah 53.2).

Milbank and Pickstock argue that the Eucharist is only present as it is broken, dispersed back into creation and history. All physical things and historical events are hallowed by it: 'trust in the Eucharist points us back towards a trust in everything, and especially the ordinary and the everyday' (*TA*, p. 111). If this is the case, however, couldn't it also be true that the ordinary and everyday, including other stories, practices and people outside the Christian fold, could teach us something about the nature of the Eucharist, and so of God? If Ward is right, the Church is crossed by lines of desire which it does not contain or control. Might not desire, so hard to capture, not only run out from the Church and its Eucharist, but back again? In other words, can Christians not learn from the desiring and questioning and making that is going on around it, and through which God might be made known – even when that activity is not visibly part of the Church?

A Church crossed by desire, a God revealed in this crossing: this might not leave us with absolute certainties, or with a vision of the whole picture. But it might be truer to the broken beauty of Christ.

Chapter summary

- Radical Orthodoxy puts the desire for God at the heart of its understanding of human life.
- It argues that desire has been captured and corrupted by sin, especially by capitalism's constant stimulation of false desires. False desire is based on lack, a craving which can never be satisfied.
- Christianity reshapes desire, directing it towards its proper end, especially through the liturgy. Eros is seen as properly part of Christian life, not something to be suppressed.

- However, we have asked whether Radical Orthodoxy's own desire is to overcome all the messiness of life, and achieve an ecstatic fusion with God, an immediate intuition or taste of the divine – and whether this is as problematic as the unreal capitalist desire it seeks to overcome.

- We have pointed out how desire is used by some Radical Orthodox writers (especially Graham Ward and Gerard Loughlin) in a more open way, to push the Christian tradition beyond its acceptance of fixed gender roles. They have also affirmed the value of same-sex unions.

- Other writers have sought to maintain traditional patterns of desire. John Milbank has tried to maintain some kind of limits to how fluid desire can be, by using the idea of affinity to suggest that some things (like men and women) naturally belong together and have a certain identity. However, he has also accepted that same-sex unions are part of God's creation.

- In the end we are left with a tension between the openness of desire, constantly shaking fixed boundaries, and the Radical Orthodox tendency to use aesthetic norms to contain desire within the Church. We have suggested that the idea of 'broken beauty' might point beyond these idealized limits.

4

Looking ahead: (not) knowing the end of the story

In telling the story of Radical Orthodoxy so far, we have concentrated on ideas of communication and connection. Language, community and desire are central to this theological vision, in which truth is an active sharing in the divine nature rather than a cold reflection of a distant God. It is a rich vision, which cannot easily be pigeon-holed. It tries to avoid the alternatives of liberalism and conservatism. It draws on Christian tradition, but denies that it advocates a premodern, backward-looking faith. It is shaped and influenced by modern and, particularly, postmodern philosophy, but it claims to avoid their pitfalls, and offer the only way to get beyond their failings.

Not surprisingly, this is a vision that has its share of tensions. It talks of a universal community of reconciliation and an inclusive Church. But it often talks in an exclusive tone, especially when rejecting the alternatives offered by other perspectives and traditions. It wants to give value back to this world, to time and matter and the body. But it seems to take refuge in highly idealized accounts of the Church and its sacraments, and to offer a kind of timeless beatific vision as the way to evade all doubt and uncertainty. It seeks to unify faith and reason. But it is criticized for dividing the Church from the world, and using assertion rather than argument.

These tensions run through the work of individual theologians as well as between them. The question of how open Christians should be to receiving truth from other traditions, or working with them on matters of common concern, remains undecided. Some writers seem more prepared to acknowledge the limitations of our knowledge of God than others, who fear that this would make

Christianity just one more story among others in the secular marketplace of ideas.

In this chapter, we will explore some of the critical comments made about Radical Orthodoxy and its individual thinkers, including some reflecting from within the movement. Many of these criticisms have already been raised in one form or another during the course of our discussion, but our aim here will be to gather them together and give them more space to breathe. In the process, we will come to some conclusions about the nature of Radical Orthodoxy, and end with some brief suggestions about other possible futures for Christian theology.

The criticisms will be organized into four sections, for easier comprehension. As always, however, we need to bear in mind that the issues raised are interconnected. The four sections will be:

- *Dualism*: does Radical Orthodoxy create damaging splits between Church and world, Christian theology and all other approaches to truth?
- *Imperialism*: is Radical Orthodoxy guilty of reinstating an oppressive form of Christian triumphalism, and does its politics do anything to further the cause of justice?
- *Rootlessness*: does Radical Orthodoxy belong anywhere, or have any accountability to real communities?
- *Monism*: is God's otherness and the integrity of the world respected in Radical Orthodoxy's theology?

Anyone who has read this far will recognize that Radical Orthodoxy would set out to deny all of these charges. It specifically seeks to avoid many of the theological and ethical problems outlined. However, the question is whether this new theology, for all its intentions and protests, still manages to get tangled up in them.

Dualism

For some critics, Radical Orthodoxy puts up walls around Christian faith, and makes theology something strictly reserved for insiders only: 'It just ghettoizes religious thought, leaving it apart from the intellectual mainstream.'[1] Radical Orthodoxy is a symptom of the way Christian theology, no longer respected in the public world and the academy, has defiantly retreated to a private, church-centred realm. It falls in step with 'the profound intellectual ghettoisation and malaise of much Christian theology'.[2]

The ghetto is the place where only insiders belong. It carries on its own customs, speaks its own language and has little if anything to do with wider society. Of course, Radical Orthodoxy might respond that ghettos were the product of modern prejudice, a false enlightenment which found no place in its grand universal vision for those who were stubbornly different and attached to their particular traditions. The Jews in particular – at least those who refused to assimilate to European 'civilization' – were kept out of sight and out of mind. That is, until anti-Semites or Nazis decided that Europe needed to be purified, cleansed of these ethnic abnormalities. Perhaps, then, it is not the ghettos that are the problem. It is the mainstream, with its demands for 'universal', clean and pure values, which is little more than a thinly disguised hatred of all those whose identities will not be submerged into a brave new world.

However, this criticism of Radical Orthodoxy can't be made to go away quite so easily. Aidan Nichols (himself a fairly conservative Roman Catholic) worries that Milbank's position in *Theology and Social Theory* results in 'the enclosure of Christian discourse and practice within a wholly separate universe of thought and action'.[3] Despite the insistence that Radical Orthodoxy wishes to overcome all forms of dualism – between God and humanity, immanence and transcendence, presence and absence, spirit and body, faith and reason – it still seems to insist on one overriding dualism: Christianity and secularism.

As we have seen, secularism is equated with paganism. It is a religion that worships violent power, that assumes that chaos and conflict, death and scarcity are at the heart of reality. Christianity tells a diametrically opposed story: of an original peaceful creation, and the reconciliation of all differences in harmony, in the Church and in the Kingdom to come. It seems that there can simply be no common ground.

Indeed, the rejection of the very notion of common ground seems close to Radical Orthodoxy's heart. There is no neutral space, language or tradition in which people can meet without their own particular commitments. That is a secular illusion, which is a cloak for a very specific faith in capitalism and the market. In the end, there is no natural or pure reason which is not part of someone's story and community and practice. For Milbank, this means that all we are left with are competing myths, a 'clash of rhetorics' (*TST*, p. 327).

Christianity is only justified by the story it tells. Radical Orthodoxy asserts that this story can dazzle and seduce us, that it has the rhetorical force to sweep us off our feet. And, like any jealous lover, it has no tolerance for rivals. It insists on our wholehearted and exclusive loyalty.

Perhaps it is no surprise, then, to find that Radical Orthodoxy has been accused of fideism and even Gnosticism.[4] Fideism is the view that a leap of faith is necessary to lead us to truth, and that this leap of faith has no possible rational justification. We simply have to believe, despite (or maybe even because of) the absurdity of the belief. Gnosticism is a term that is used to refer to a variety of Christian and non-Christian groups rejected as heretical by the Church in the first centuries of the Christian era (variants of which have arisen from time to time since). Two general aspects of their belief systems are relevant here. The first is their insistence on gnosis, special knowledge which would secure the soul's passage from this world to the fullness of heaven. This knowledge was mystical, or esoteric – hidden words and names and symbols. The second aspect of their philosophy was a pervasive dualism. They tended to believe that the physical world and our bodies were evil, the creations of a lesser deity, in which our eternal, spiritual souls were trapped. Salvation lay in releasing the soul or divine spark from the prison of the body, to rejoin the fullness of the true God from which it has been separated. Christian Gnostics typically saw Jesus as a divine saviour bringing hidden knowledge of God, who only appeared to be human, but in reality was purely spiritual or angelic.

At first glance, the idea that Radical Orthodoxy could be accused of either fideism or Gnosticism seems bizarre. For one thing, it does not seek to abolish reason, but to take away the division between reason and faith. Reason too depends on divine illumination. Truth is not a dry formula but an active sharing in God's nature. Radical Orthodox writers tend to be critical of theologians like Karl Barth, who wished to keep faith and revelation so pure that they were divorced from the world, forcing their way in from the outside. Against Barth's fideism, Radical Orthodoxy proposes a more holistic vision. As for Gnosticism, the value placed by Radical Orthodoxy on the material creation is only part of its attempt to get away from all dualisms.

However, two factors mean that the movement still has a case to answer:

- We have noted the aesthetic dimension of its theology. Paul Janz points out this tendency for Radical Orthodoxy to create free-floating pictures of truth, which are not rooted in any subject, or any appeal to reason or historical interpretation. After all, if reason and philosophy are wholly emptied out into theology, what is left for reason to do? The truth is just something we either see or do not see, depending upon whether we let ourselves be overwhelmed by the force of the picture that is painted. Any reference to identities or substances or realities beyond the picture are ruled out of court. And this leads to a 'gnostic Christology', in the sense that Christ simply becomes part of a freewheeling literary myth, with no connection to the empirical world. The only authority this theology can claim is a secret, esoteric one, 'the special "intellectual intuition" or the prophetic ingenuity of the few'.[5]
- The flip side of this collapsing of all reality into a literary myth is the dualistic claim that all other myths are evil, dark and violent. If there is nothing but rhetorics, and if those rhetorics are in ceaseless conflict, then there is nothing but violence. Secularism or capitalism becomes the bogeyman, wholly evil and unredeemable. But when Radical Orthodoxy makes such huge claims for the Church and the Eucharist as the sole place where we can be in the truth and manifest God's nature, then it seems as if all non-Christian stories and traditions must be tarred with the same brush. As Milbank puts it, Christianity is

'not just different, but [is] *the* difference from all other cultural systems, which it exposes as threatened by incipient nihilism' (*TST*, p. 381).

When Radical Orthodoxy raises the bar of its claims, these criticisms start to look more justified. When Milbank argues that philosophy began as a secularizing force, this allows him to conclude that theology must 'entirely evacuate' it leaving it nothing to do or see (*WMS*, p. 50).

The problem is partly that of making such huge generalizations in the first place. However, such tactics also put theology in a strange predicament. If theology can only come into being as human words and images and stories in response to God, then it cannot be wholly divorced from other human ways of conceiving the world. Languages are not self-contained wholes. They grow by adapting and absorbing. They shape the world, but the world exerts pressure back upon language. Stories are interlinked, open to being told and retold differently in different contexts. Even grammars are not static and cut off from the changing world.

None of this means that all stories are the same, or that there is some magical way of identifying 'reality' apart from our language and stories. However, it does imply that our language is always in a relationship of dialogue and questioning with what is beyond it. Any particular tradition cannot wash its hands of all the rest, in a blasé and sweeping way. As John Hoffmeyer puts it, 'The very idea of the preservation of a discrete, unsullied narrative tradition in the face of other traditions is a misunderstanding of the nature of stories' (*ITP*, p. 16).

For Hoffmeyer, this means that Radical Orthodoxy needs to offer a more sympathetic reading of modern philosophy, and of Christian theology's various attempts to engage with it. This does not mean uncritically accepting the assumptions and arguments put forward, but acknowledging that problems of knowledge, reference, authority and realism simply can't be wished away.

Milbank seems to acknowledge this when he responds to some of his more conservative Christian critics. He suggests that they see Radical Orthodoxy as too modern and too liberal, because it often takes very general ideas (like gift, peace, beauty) and then says that these things can only be saved if they are given a Christian gloss. Contrary to appearances, Radical Orthodoxy makes the specifically Christian content of these ideas come second. Milbank doesn't attempt to deny that there is some truth in this. He recognizes:

> if there are no 'general' notions uncontaminated by the contingencies of language and circumstance, then equally there is no pure concrete given starting point uncontaminated by general abstract notions. Thus the concreteness of the gospels is also a mosaic of inherited general and vague notions and images, and there is no sheerly Christian language which will not be somewhat understood by non Christians. (*ROCE*, p. 37)

However, this admission is not as surprising as it sounds. It is still grudging, conceding that non-Christians may understand a little of what Christians are saying, but not really reflecting on the fact that Christians have something to learn and receive from other languages and ideas which may not have been entirely anticipated by their own theology. It also does not deal with the fact that Radical Orthodoxy believes that language is far more than abstract ideas. Language does things, it shapes the world into a coherent pattern. So even if the secular world has some of the right words, it still presumably lacks any idea of what to do with them, because it is stuck with a view of language as lifeless labels or tools of force.

Radical Orthodoxy has a strong story of how things went wrong with the world, often starting with Duns Scotus. The problem with such a simple story is that it becomes an excuse not to think through the issues themselves. Duns Scotus or Kant or Derrida can be wheeled out. They all essentially have the same sickness, which is trying to subject God's being to our forms of knowledge, and separating us from the divine in the process. But such grand explanatory stories risk becoming shallow, and divide the world up in dualistic fashion between the elect who know the mind of God and all others who are apologists for the devil. As Rosemary Radford Ruether says of Stephen Long's version of this history:

Long's method of thought exaggerates Western history of thought into a dualism of narrative truth, goodness and beauty (Aquinas and an idealized Church located in a utopian moment of undetermined historicity) on the one hand, and fallacious modernity that justifies an alienated self that leads to nihilism on the other.

(*ITP*, p. 78)

Gavin Hyman reinforces the point. He argues that Milbank 'confronts us with a straightforward antinomy: either theology will "position" other discourses or else other discourses will "position" theology. This blatant dichotomy is simply assumed and taken for granted.'[6]

Why does this split come about? Jeffrey Stout argues that much of the new traditionalism in theology, including Radical Orthodoxy, is based on a resentment of the secular. He draws a distinction between secularism, an ideology that is hostile to religion, and secularization, the process whereby the authority of theology and the Church is no longer taken as the automatic basis for political arrangements. A secular society does not need to be run on secularist lines. It can still leave room for religious believers to put forward their distinctive positions and beliefs. Their religion is not excluded, it simply cannot be taken for granted as the truth everyone shares and submits to. Stout argues that 'this just means that the age of theocracy is over, not that the anti-Christ has taken control of the political sphere'.[7]

Stout therefore rejects Radical Orthodoxy's claim that secular political arrangements are inevitably driven by the evil genie of secularism. Secularism, for Stout, is a failed ideology, which claimed that religion was disappearing in the face of reason and enlightenment. A secular society is a more flexible and ambiguous reality, which in its best forms aims at mature, democratic processes of debate. It does not exclude people holding religious positions, or arguing on the basis of a religious world-view, but they do so with an awareness that maturity and openness demand that other world-views are listened to with respect.

The problem with Radical Orthodoxy's lack of such respect is that it polarizes debate. It fosters the view that religion works by an entirely different logic or grammar to any other language game. Its effect can be to confirm religion's withdrawal to the margins, and give credence to secularist assumptions that religious faith has nothing to offer public debate. As Stout puts it, 'radical orthodoxy's critique of the secular tends, under current circumstances, to reinforce the sort of boundary-drawing it officially opposes'. The combination of nostalgia and utopianism in Radical Orthodoxy, without any more engaged political theology to supplement them, 'threaten to condemn the world to utter darkness'. Stout concludes in withering fashion: 'From within radical orthodoxy's refuge of aggressive like-mindedness, prophetic denunciations of the secular "other" and the unmasking of liberal theological error ritually reinforce the enclave boundary, rather than healing the world.'[8] Faced with this indictment, producing texts in which Milbank and others talk about the Church's open boundaries is not enough. Such idealistic and abstract openness needs to offer a more concrete hospitality.

For Stout, part of this involves not only a more measured and generous view of secular societies, it also means paying more attention to the virtues which have shaped the move to democracy and social justice in those societies. By examining some of the key figures in the development of American democracy, Stout finds that there are religious and rational traditions which aim to shape people's characters, enabling them to participate fully in public life. The fact that these traditions are not always respected, that democracy can become oppressive and servile to vested economic and national interests does not invalidate Stout's point. In fact, it reinforces his view that what is required is a deeper engagement with democracy on the part of religious people, so its ideals and virtues can be lived out – not resentment, condemnation and withdrawal.

If society is diminished by the tactics adopted by Radical Orthodoxy, so, some argue, is the Church itself. In his reflection on *Theology and Social Theory*, Rowan Williams states that 'What I am concerned to keep in view is the danger of setting the common life of the Church too dramatically apart from the temporal ways in which the good is realized in a genuinely contingent world.'[9] The contingency – the messiness and ambiguity – of the world disappears from view if a simple good-versus-evil model is imposed upon it. And the Church is then set adrift, made into an unreal utopia.

Again, this is not Radical Orthodoxy's intention. We have seen how Milbank and others deny that the Church is utopian or perfect. However, by emphasizing so strongly the Church's divine nature, and by focusing on the Eucharist as the place where all doubt is banished and God and humanity are fused together, a different impression is given.

There are wider theological issues at stake here. If faith and reason, nature and grace are not separate, as Radical Orthodoxy maintains, then it seems to follow that God will be made manifest outside the Church. If there is no perfect story, and no perfect community, if our apprehension of truth is always partial, then it makes sense for Christian theology to look for God's nature to be made known in a plurality of forms of association and endeavour.

Stephen Long's view that the Church should be seen as infallible is difficult to match with the divided state of the churches and their evident involvement in corruption, violence and erroneous beliefs about the nature of the world. More positively, Catholic theologians have pointed to the integrity of reason and the work given to philosophy. Reformed theologians have affirmed the validity and purpose of institutions other than the Church. Neither group has set up arbitrary divisions between faith and reason, Church and world, or assumed that there is any part of creation which has meaning apart from its relationship to God. But given the questionable nature of our vision, they find reason to resist setting theology up as 'queen of the sciences', or making the Church the sole witness and realization of the Kingdom of God.

In practice, of course, Radical Orthodoxy does use tools of argument and reason. Its books are published on the open market. Its supporters are often part of theological faculties which do not have rigid confessional bases. In other words, Radical Orthodoxy is involved in addressing the world, in terms the world can (at least partially!) understand. There is no pure 'Christian' story or mode of thinking. But this is not incorporated into and allowed to influence some of the movement's more exclusive pronouncements.

Radical Orthodoxy's tendency to sidestep the questionable nature of its own theology and sources of authority has led commentators to dismiss it as 'sophisticated fundamentalism', as 'an exercise in self-protective false consciousness' or an example of 'magical consciousness',[10] which ignores the real, material conditions of life. Marcella Althaus-Reid puts the point graphically, in reflecting on the relationship between Radical Orthodoxy's idealized view of the Church and the reality of life in the slums of Latin America: 'are liturgical acts independent of mundane things belonging to the sphere of production, such as a house, or the searching for stale bread in the bins?' (*ITP*, p. 110).

The theological question here is does Radical Orthodoxy truly take seriously the materiality of creation? And does it have an adequate doctrine of the God who became incarnate in Christ? If, as Janz and others have suggested, Radical Orthodoxy tends to dissolve any reference to the world around us into a pure, aesthetic intuition of God, has it really done justice to orthodox ideas of the creation, the incarnation, the cross and resurrection?

Althaus-Reid's point is worth noting: 'Liberation theology takes account of the fragility of God in history, while radical orthodoxy seems to have a God-ideal, outside failures and plateaus of destitution' (*ITP*, p. 111). Despite its protestations, does Radical Orthodoxy offer us a God untouched by the world, a God who uses Church and Eucharist to dominate and overwhelm all opposition? Is this an imperialistic theology after all?

Imperialism

According to Althaus-Reid, Radical Orthodoxy remains 'deeply colonial' and Elina Vuola equates it with 'radical eurocentrism' (*ITP*, p. 112 and p. 75). Its criticisms of liberation theology have certainly angered some, who see them as another example of the patronizing superiority and conservatism of Anglo-American theology from the global North. However, as we have seen, Radical Orthodoxy does claim to be socialist, and directs much of its energy into anti-capitalist arguments. Are its critics getting it wrong?

There does seem to be a problem of communication, as the concerns and engagements of theologians based in the UK and USA do not always map onto those in the developing world. The issues thrown up by secularization, consumerism, individualism and western philosophies of knowledge and selfhood give a particular context to Radical Orthodoxy, which can make it seem academic and out of touch in other settings.

However, there are also significant questions of substance at stake. As we have seen, Rowan Williams questions Milbank's version of the Christian story, because it seems to cut out all the difficult and complicated ways the Church exists in relationship to a contingent world. And he adds, 'how might a woman tell this story as a story of peace or promise?'[11]

There are two related points here. First, Williams is making the point that all stories are contested. Even when we are dealing with the fundamental stories that shape a religious community, there are always different perspectives and voices. The Church is not monochrome. It has existed in many forms across cultures and history. This does not necessarily mean that it cannot hold differences in harmony. But, as a matter of fact, we know that the churches have been affected by conflict from the beginning of the Christian era until the present day. We cannot assume in advance that these differences can quickly be resolved into harmony. It is easy to talk about 'the' Christian story in the singular, when in fact Christian tradition is made of many stories, told in many accents. The difficult work of listening, interpretation and dialogue cannot be set to one side.

The second point is that the ability to tell a story and make truth claims heard is partly a question of power. The fact that Williams asks what the Christian story and the story of the Church would be like as told by a woman is significant. It reminds us that the voices of women have often not been heard within the Church, and that they have been denied public sacramental roles and positions of ecclesial authority. And this has been bound up with deep strands of patriarchal thinking, in which women have been labelled as secondary to men, sources of impurity and temptation, ruled by passions, and therefore required to submit to male control.

On this telling of the story, the Church has been part of the problem. Even if theologians now renounce sexism and other oppressive cultural practices, how can they claim that the Church can be elevated as the uniquely privileged place where God and humanity meet? Shouldn't they admit that the story of the Church is a broken one, which at times requires challenge from within and without – which also implies that perhaps aspects of truth and justice are being revealed beyond its borders? Don't 'secular' movements claim a lot of credit for putting issues of sexism, racism and homophobia on the agenda, for example, and for achieving other political goals, such as fairer treatment for workers, good health care and universal education? The Church may well have been part of all of these movements. But it has not walked alone (and sometimes it has walked in the opposite direction).

As Debra Dean Murphy points out, the Church cannot speak from a position of purity: 'Christianity itself is implicated in the kinds of power from which Milbank is trying to dissociate it.'[12] It is with these kinds of considerations in mind that Mark Chapman takes issue with Daniel Bell's arguments (shared by others in the Radical Orthodox fold) that the Church is the true politics: 'If politics is solely to be lived in the Church, then what happens to those of other religions, or who see the Church as the historic perpetrator of violence and abuse to minorities and to women who refuse to join?'[13]

The point is echoed by contributors to *Interpreting the Post-modern*. For Vuola, Bell's position is based upon a 'blame the victim' approach, which criticizes the poor for struggling for their rights, and asks them to practise an idealized forgiveness. She asks 'how exactly should poor people "forgive capitalism," women "sexism," nonwhites "racism" and slavery, and so forth? Histor-ically seen, the Christian Church and its dominant theology have been some of the legitimizers and defenders of all those systems' (*ITP*, p. 74).

Lisa Isherwood also attacks Bell for sentimentalizing forgiveness, and making suffering into something redemptive, thereby condemning the poor to accept their lot. This, she argues results from 'an overemphasis on the metaphysical and a downplaying of the material', recalling the charge that Radical Orthodoxy slides into Gnosticism. Indeed, Isherwood goes further, expressing a concern that the Christian Right is reasserting the imperial Christ that destroyed local cultures, and that 'Bell and many of those involved in the radical orthodoxy movement are allies in this Christo-fascist agenda' (*ITP*, p. 173).

There is a danger that these criticisms become so extreme that they become absurd, reducing their target to a one-dimensional enemy to be attacked (much as Milbank and Blond associate eco-theology and secular society respectively with fascism). Calling someone a fascist or a Nazi rarely helps to advance debate (and risks trivializing the threat posed by actual fascists and Nazis). Radical Orthodoxy's opposition to western capitalism, its promotion of socialism and its arguments against the colonial mentality behind some apparently 'liberal' theologies should not be ignored, whether one agrees with them or not.

However, the underlying theological concerns expressed by Isherwood and others need to be taken seriously. Chief among these is the question of transcendence and immanence, and the relationship of God to the world. At this point, it is worth summarizing the potential difficulty faced by Radical Orthodoxy.

- On the one hand, we have seen that Radical Orthodoxy opposes dualisms, which pit spirit against matter, faith against reason, God against humanity. Milbank even writes of the boundary between creator and creation being crossed by the incarnation. Modern philosophy – like that of Kant – looks as if it is being modest, because it refuses to go beyond the limits of what we can know. However, Radical Orthodoxy says this is a false modesty, because modern philosophy arrogantly assumes that it knows where the limits of knowledge can be drawn, and religiously rejects any analogical relationship between God and humanity. In contrast, Christianity affirms that the infinite is always revealed in and through the finite, the worldly, the sensuous.

- On the other hand, Radical Orthodoxy erects its own limits around how God can be known. Because Christianity is '*the* difference' from all other cultural systems, it views everything secular as founded upon nothingness and violence. The secular – all that is not-Church – is the immanent which has cut itself off from the transcendent. The consequence of this is that only in Christianity, its Church and Eucharist, do the immanent and transcendent meet. Radical Orthodoxy therefore ends up making a huge assumption about when and where God can be met. It does not succeed in healing the rift between the transcendent and the immanent, because it denies the possibility of God being present in worldliness, except in a very abstract and idealized way in the Church. And the upshot of this is that it makes the Church into a transcendent reality, separate from the rest of history and culture. From its lofty vantage point, the Church claims immediate contact with God, and an ability to dictate meaning and truth to the world.

With factors like these in mind, James Hanvey expresses his concern at Radical Orthodoxy's 'failure to substantiate its epistemology other than by asserting it' (*ROCE*, p. 162). Writers like Blond assert that 'epistemology' – the theory of knowledge – is a modern disease, since only in modernity has the thinking subject been cut off from the transcendent and started worrying about whether it really knows anything (first-year philosophy students will be familiar with questions like 'Am I a brain in a vat?' 'How do I know other people exist?' and so on). However, Radical Orthodoxy still claims knowledge – indeed it can even claim to know the mind of God. And it has to give a critical account of this when questioned.

According to Hanvey, the failure to come up with such reasoned responses threatens to undermine Radical Orthodoxy's whole project. Its intention is to overcome the emptiness of secular nihilism, and its underlying love affair with brute power and violence. But Radical Orthodoxy's own position arguably produces the same result. One picture of the world is forcefully asserted as the truth, and all other views are seen as locked in warfare with it. Does this mean that the real motivating drive of this theology's interpretation of the world is the will to power? If this is so, then 'far from addressing modernity's nihilism, Radical Orthodoxy depends upon it' (*ROCE*, p. 167). It still separates God from all worldly knowledge, and then constructs Radical Orthodoxy as the ultimate means to secure (and consume) that object. Gavin Hyman agrees, pointing to the 'inescapable violence' with which Milbank has to assert his story of Christianity at war with the secular.[14]

Rivera argues that the problem is not so much the stress on the fact of the transcendence of God, but the *way* in which transcendence is understood. Transcendence is a useful way of preserving the otherness of God, stopping us from thinking that we can define and own God. However, when it is set in opposition to immanence, when the secular is assumed to be a godless void, then transcendence becomes a means of claiming power and privileged insight. Pickstock and others take certain actions or phrases, and, detaching them from their historical context, give them the power to put us directly in touch with God and take us out of the world. They lose patience with the complexity of such communications – the potential that any theological language or liturgy can 'fail to mean' when used in a context of domination or exclusion (*ITP*, pp. 137–8).

This reminds us of Althaus-Reid's charge that Radical Orthodoxy has a 'God-ideal, outside failures and plateaus of destitution' (*ITP*, p. 111). Milbank in particular has insisted on a traditional understanding of God as 'pure act', with no unfulfilled potential. There can be no lack in God, only fullness, if God is not to be made into the sickly mirror image of our own striving. Milbank therefore strongly opposes any idea that God can suffer, an idea which has been popular in much modern theology, even though it represents a break with classical Christian tradition.

For Greek thought, God has to be thought of as impassable, unable to be affected by anything outside him. To think God could change, or could suffer, would be a denial of his divine and perfect nature. God is not dependent upon anything else, is infinite and eternal, and cannot be defined by any reality other than his own nature. This idea was taken up in Christian theology, with the curious result that theologians have to argue that Christ suffered in his human nature, but not in his divine nature.

Dissatisfaction with this approach, particularly in the twentieth century, was driven by political and ethical concerns. If God were truly compassionate, and in solidarity with those who suffered, then the idea of his impassability at least had to be revisited. It could be argued that God allowed himself to become vulnerable to suffering, allowed creation to affect him, out of his own free, creative and loving will.

For Milbank, this reduces God too much to our level, making him a bigger and better version of a person. It is based on the idea, derived from Duns Scotus, that our being and God's are essentially the same. But this merger of God and humanity stops God really being able to liberate us from suffering. God is just caught up in the same mess as us. What's worse, those theologies which go further and talk of creation as God's body, rob creation of its independent life, and make God into a big divine ego, worrying about the state of his physique. In contrast, Milbank holds that God 'experiences nothing of evil . . . does not in any way suffer, acts without fear in the world' (*WMS*, p. 229). Only so can God overcome our slavery to death.

However, it is far from clear that all ideas of God's compassion need result in this kind of caricature of the sympathetic counsellor in the sky. For God to allow himself to be affected by creation can be seen as an expression of divine freedom, as strengthening the dignity and worth of creation. God takes the risk of creating life other than his own, life which is fragile, mortal and tempted to evil.

And the alternative offered by Milbank has its own problems. Commenting on Aquinas' understanding of the incarnation, Milbank states that God can have no real relation to either creation in general or to Jesus' humanity in particular, because 'there is no outside of God' (*BR*, p. 73). God's self-sufficiency cannot be diminished.

This view makes it difficult to conceive what God's compassion and love mean, or how Christ is actually a unified person, rather than two separate natures loosely stuck together. If love is ignorant of any vulnerability, difference, risk or response, it begins to look like an indifferent force. Indeed, Milbank goes so far in arguing that the incarnation makes no real difference to God, that he says that God cannot really be said to forgive us at all, since God is not affected by sin, and simply keeps on giving the original gift of creation.

Similarly, it can be difficult to see how God has any kind of relationship to what is not God. All differences seem to be somehow contained within God, so that the destiny of creation and humanity appears to be that of being merged into the divine (again much as Gnosticism believed we were saved when our separate divine sparks became one with the divine fullness again). There is nothing that is really outside God. Creation – for all the value Radical Orthodoxy claims to give it – seems to be either an illusion or an unfortunate interlude before the soul finds its true home.

Of course, in speaking of God, all language must be critically examined. The idea of God suffering, or that there can be an 'outside' and an 'inside' to God is clearly analogical or metaphorical language. However, given that this is the only language we have to speak of God, simply to deny it on the basis of Greek metaphysics seems arbitrary. More importantly, it risks projecting an image of God something like Aristotle's 'unmoved mover', who keeps the world in motion without ever being moved himself. And it is valid to ask what the relationship is between this deity and the jealous, desiring, angry, tender, passionate, embodied God of the Bible and Christian devotion.

Does the God-ideal of Radical Orthodoxy really leave room for the failures, ambiguities and compromises of history, including the history of the Church? The fact that this question can even be asked reveals an uncertainty as to how this theology's claims really connect with the concrete realities of life, or respect the mystery and freedom of creation.

Rootlessness

The Church is clearly not an optional extra for Radical Orthodox (and much other postliberal) theology. Christianity is a social project, a community event. Only in community can the incarnation be more than just a theory or a past event. In the Church, it becomes the heartbeat of a people's way of life, promising universal reconciliation and the harmonious blending of differences.

However, we have noted the tensions that call this vision of the Church into question. Gavin D'Costa sums up the essential issue when he writes that Radical Orthodoxy 'is a church theology with no accountability to any real church'.[15] In an earlier critique of *Theology and Social Theory*, Aidan Nichols underlines the point by asking 'What Church *is* this to which Milbank makes appeal?'[16]

The idealization of the Church, and its uncertain relationship to the actual churches of history, has been discussed in previous chapters. The Church in Radical Orthodoxy acts as a buffer against individualism, and as a bridge between the transcendence of God and the earthly reality of created life. However, when the Church becomes an ideal, an abstraction, it is hard to see how it can perform either of those functions.

The Church cannot save people from individualism if it is the product of an individual theologian's imagination. Milbank is honest enough to doubt openly whether any existing Church and Christian practice really lives out the gospel as he describes it. However, his claim that the Church's task seems to fall upon the theologian's head appears to devalue everything else that he says about the need for the Church as the body that continues or extends the incarnate presence of God in the world. Is the theologian now the incarnation of God? Are theological ideas enough to give God body in the world?

This disappearance of the Church from real, shared life also makes it hard to understand how it can successfully bring God and people together in the strong form which Radical Orthodoxy's doctrine of the Eucharist implies. The suspicion is that 'transubstantiation' actually empties created signs and material reality of their content and substance, overwhelming them with God's unearthly presence. When everything depends on the specific event of the divine gift, enacted out in the Eucharist, created things have no abiding reality. Radical Orthodoxy claims that this saves them from dropping into the void. But it also threatens to empty the world of its own inherent potential for meaning and life.

It is not that Radical Orthodoxy is wrong to see the Eucharist as revealing the sacramental nature of creation. It is just that it claims too much when it asserts that only one theory of how the Eucharist does this is possible for Christians, and that it is only because of the Eucharist that we can give any meaning to anything else. Just as stories and languages are not pure and self-contained, so communities and their rituals are also connected to a wider world of social interaction and material reality. This does not mean that the Eucharist loses its uniqueness, or its capacity to reveal, but it does imply that the world can help us to understand the meaning of the Eucharist, as well as the other way round. And it suggests that no one theory of the sacrament will say all that there is to be said.[17]

A rootless Church goes together with a rootless Christ. If the Church becomes an abstraction, this suggests that the incarnation itself might have been turned into a spiritualized and disembodied self-contradiction. Ross Thompson comments sharply: 'The Christ of Radical Orthodoxy does appear to be more Word than flesh.'[18] Reno agrees: 'Authority shifts out of the particularity of word and sacrament into a supervening theory or concept.'[19]

We saw how Stephen Long noted that Milbank's Jesus was without substance. However, Long does go on to argue that this doesn't necessarily mean that Milbank has abandoned orthodoxy, only that he seeks to make it more dynamic, more embedded in story and language. Making Christ a poetic reality has to be understood in the context of Milbank's account of poetic creativity, in which our making and divine giving meet. Language itself is not a dead collection of signs pointing to facts, but a living web of relationship: 'Human language becomes a participation in God's infinite plenitude' (*DE*, p. 253). Or, as Milbank himself puts it, 'our linguistic expression mirrors the divine creative act' (*WMS*, p. 29).

However, this only sharpens the questions laid at Radical Orthodoxy's door. If the Church is a work in process, and if revelation is conditional on our (presumably imperfect) acts of creativity, then it becomes hard to justify claims that the Church is inevitably the true politics, the exemplary community and so on.

We've seen how Milbank and others do admit the imperfection of the Church, but find it hard to work this reality back into their theories of what the Church should be like. The contingent nature of language acts as a check on such theories, Milbank argues (*WMS*, p. 29). There is no getting away from history and culture. But how then can the Church continue to claim to have the key to *all* language and meaning? How can Christians claim that their story withstands *all* criticism?

The idea of the Church as a fiction can work both ways. It can draw attention to the particular ways in which human beings have imagined and created the Church, and to the ways in which the Church could have been different. Or it can pull the Church away from this real process of making, and allow the theologian to invent a new Church to fit his or her vision. This is the charge made by some critics of Radical Orthodoxy: that it effectively has no home, and has to invent a place of belonging. It is therefore an academic exercise, which is not answerable to any community and has no means of testing its claims for orthodoxy against any authority (*ROCE*, pp. 8–9).

Monism

Monism is the view that there is only one single reality, one sort of 'stuff' that makes up everything. It might seem odd to accuse a theology of both dualism and monism, but there is a consistency to this criticism. When Radical Orthodoxy divides the world into two (pagan or secular versus Christian), it denies all essential reality to one side of this partition. Just as Augustine argued that evil had no reality in itself, but was a privation, a lack, a falling away from goodness, so the secular is derided as baseless, empty and illusory. So, in the end, there is only one reality.

'Christ is absorbed into the Church',[20] and if this is not enough, Simon Taylor points to the 'virtual equation of God and theology' he sees in Radical Orthodoxy.[21] Thanks to the way language is understood, the power of the true storyteller is no merely human one. It is the power of God in the world. As Christ becomes a poetic reality, so Frederick Bauerschmidt (a contributor to *Radical Orthodoxy*) worries that Milbank turns Christianity into a wholly linguistic phenomenon.[22]

The inability to hear any voice but its own, the inability truly to make room for the 'other', seems to be an accusation that lies behind many of the other criticisms we have already examined. For Marcella Althaus-Reid, 'There is no sense of exteriority in radical orthodoxy' (*ITP*, p. 112). And, as Gavin Hyman argues, Milbank's way of setting up the debate between theology and the secular 'seems to *promote* an agonistic and violent strategy that eradicates a genuine commitment to difference'.[23]

On the surface, Radical Orthodoxy sees Christianity as the one story able truly to respect and harmonize differences. In practice, it is forgetful of difference, whenever it confuses its own telling of the story with 'Christianity' itself as some kind of pure essence or master story. However, as Hyman points out, 'theology (and indeed, every other discourse) must always be supplemented by other discourses'.[24] Why else does Radical Orthodoxy use those general, vague ideas of peace, the gift, narrative and so on, unless they were needed to position the Christian story in a new way, relevant to our postmodern times? Doesn't Milbank claim that the Church itself had to 'invent' doctrines to clarify the Gospels and make them more attractive?

From one direction, then, Radical Orthodoxy is accused of denying everything that is not Christianity and the Church, using them to master and subdue all opponents. From the other direction, it is charged with dissolving the identity of Christ and the Church into a highly speculative philosophical story of things, in which it takes the role of the all-seeing narrator.

The doctrine of participation, for example, has been questioned by Reformed theologians, who prefer to talk of a covenant relationship between God and creation. They worry that 'participation' removes the difference between God and humanity, trespassing on God's otherness and holiness. The doctrine of participation is particularly important, because it is the theme that seeks to harmonize everything else. Language, the Church, theology, the Eucharist – all share in God's nature. However, Radical Orthodoxy's insistence that its story alone can tell us where these harmonies are heard is based on selective listening, the drowning out of all other melodies save one. Its poetry is beautiful, but is it true? Or is it like the poet described by Kierkegaard, 'who conceals profound anguish in his heart but whose lips are so formed that as sighs and cries pass over them they sound like beautiful music'?[25] Can Radical Orthodoxy give voice to the anguish of the world, without burying them under its own romanticized arts?

Some of the criticisms of Radical Orthodoxy which we have been exploring were anticipated by Graham Ward in his response to *Theology and Social Theory* back in 1992. He questions the status of Milbank's claims to be able to tell the Christian master story, asking 'is there only *one* Christian story?'[26] Behind these claims, Ward suspects that a kind of Christian imperialism may be lurking. The only way to avoid this, it seems, is an awareness that such stories cannot force their truth upon us: 'if we accept the correlation between our knowledge and our stories and that this book is a story, an invention, then there is no position available from which to claim that this story is right or wrong.'[27]

Ward returned to this question of the status of Radical Orthodoxy's claims in his contribution to the dialogue with Roman Catholic theologians. He describes the movement as a 'cultural politics'. It is not homogenous, but it is woven together by a theme. It 'reads the contemporary world through the Christian tradition, weaving it into the narrative of that tradition'. Ward is clear that, though there is a basic grammar of Christian orthodoxy, it is not monochrome: 'there is not *one* Christian tradition' (*ROCE*, p. 106). And Radical Orthodoxy is not merely counter-cultural and sectarian. It engages with and even learns from the culture around it (*ROCE*, p. 104).

For Ward, Radical Orthodoxy must be aware of its own context. It is not rootless, 'for commitment to specific ecclesial communities is the beginning and the end of its reflections'. Its truth claims are not nostalgia, or mere rhetoric, but claims about the nature of reality and being. However, they must always be accompanied by a 'healthy agnosticism' because of theology's awareness of human fragility and conditioning (*ROCE*, p. 110).

Earlier in the essay we have been quoting from, Ward asks what is needed to make a belief believable in the modern world. First, he answers that we have to accept that some authority is legitimate, to place some trust in a person, institution, text or whatever. Second, we have to assume that the world has a shape, that it can be known. And, third, we have to assume that we can represent the world's shape, picture and communicate it transparently. Unfortunately, we are constantly forced to question all of these assumptions. There is a gap between what we are supposed to trust and the ways we are supposed to establish that trust. Those who are trying to convince us of their truth have to enter this gap with various means of persuasion. Radical Orthodoxy reads the signs of the times, and has taken the opportunity offered by our contemporary loss of faith in liberalism. In a sense, it is swimming with the cultural tide.

Ward's version of Radical Orthodoxy is more self-critical and open to being 'positioned' by other discourses, at least to some extent. But this places it in an uncomfortable relationship with other versions of Radical Orthodoxy, which do not seem to have any problem claiming to run rings around secularism, do without anything that is not theology, and perceive the truth transparently and directly in Church and sacrament. The story told by Ward can only be told by someone who has already acknowledged that the 'big story' of Radical Orthodoxy is as fragile and limited as any other human reality. The result is a theology that cannot be so totally divorced from liberalism as Ward himself might like.

The 'healthy agnosticism' which Ward embraces suggests that some of the self-assurance of Radical Orthodoxy needs to be questioned. But it also suggests a very different style of theology, which might better be able to answer some of the criticisms and challenges we have encountered in this chapter. It is with that possibility in mind that I offer some concluding reflections.

Dialogue, compassion, unknowing: theology's futures

Radical Orthodoxy is undoubtedly a bold vision, and has done a great deal to stimulate debate, raise the profile of theology in the academy and provide a boost to the self-confidence of at least some Christian theologians. Theology no longer needs to hide away in the corner, apologizing for its existence in the academy and wider public world. Indeed, it can take on a newly critical, even belligerent tone as it unmasks the pretensions of secular ideologies to sweep religion under the carpet.

Much of this is welcome, and there are subtleties in Radical Orthodoxy's key texts which can easily be missed. In the end, however, it risks painting itself into a corner. It rejects dialogue with the secular. It reduces philosophy to the status of theology's handmaid. It lumps all alternative positions under labels like 'paganism' and 'nihilism'.

However, a certain encounter with worldliness, and the emptiness or questionability of our own constructions of reality is unavoidable for theology. If there is no purely secular language, neither is there a purely theological language. The engagement with what is not theology – whether philosophy or liberalism or paganism itself – is not something that can be rejected, because it has always already begun. The very terms used by Christian orthodoxy were honed in Greek philosophy, and Radical Orthodoxy's debt to Plato is clear. As Milbank admits, it uses general ideas of narrative, poetry and so on, in order to tease out what the Christian stories might mean and what their status is for us today.

Neither the Christian story, nor the ways in which that story is articulated through doctrine, can be sealed off from other stories, theories and discourses. Those other voices echo through Christian telling, such that the Church and its story themselves become plural and multifaceted. To suppose otherwise is naive. It is a political move, which is only secured by trying to impose a fixed, idealized framework upon how the story is told. But that framework is invented, and disputed.

Radical Orthodoxy is not unaware of all of this, of course. It takes advantage of the postmodern moment to declare that it needs no foundation, that its story can only be justified by its aesthetic appeal. But beneath the embracing of postmodernity's aesthetic, a will to power can be detected. Force is deployed. War between different rhetorics is the ultimate reality. To hold one's position in this conflict it seems one must appeal to things that look very much like new foundations, however much they are disguised: the perfect Church, the God who consumes all otherness, the story which leaves nothing out, the Eucharist which fuses us to God.

Radical Orthodoxy cannot be blamed for failing to deliver a perfect theology, in which all these difficult questions of starting points, identity and authority are resolved. It can be charged with pretending to offer such a resolution, based on nothing more than a sleight of hand which equates orthodoxy with postmodernism.

In many ways, Radical Orthodoxy replicates the sins it professes to transcend. It accuses conservatives of introducing revelation into the world from the outside, and yet it cannot avoid detaching Christianity, its Church and liturgy from any worldly relationships. It pillories liberals for letting secular disciplines come first, with theology only as a gloss. And yet its own speculative doctrines play a huge a priori role in shaping what can be experienced and understood of God and the world. Postmodernism is faulted for its nihilism. But Radical Orthodoxy has no grounds for asserting its own story of peace and harmony – a story which can sound like a tale of suppression of and indifference to all that is other.

These shortcomings are sometimes remarked within the movement itself. Graham Ward in particular shows a greater reticence and awareness of the provisional nature of theology than some of his companions. Without returning to simple liberalism, he remains aware of the inevitably limited cultural context in which the gospel is received and proclaimed.

Ward's criticisms of Karl Barth eerily echo those often made of Radical Orthodoxy. Barth, he says, fails to reflect fully on the way Christ is always interpreted, mediated through culture. As a result, Barth's theology reflects modernity's split consciousness, turning it into an attack on the secular which is dualistic: 'The world is so lost, so secularised, so ignorant of God that both Christ and subsequently a theology of Christ operate above and beyond such a world, in contradistinction to it.'[28] There is an 'idealist tendency' which 'is amplified when theology appeals only to its own theological resources in order to define itself'.[29]

In contrast, Ward is clear that Christian theology cannot avoid apologetics. It must engage with the languages and cultures around it, or it will end up talking only to itself. This is not an abandonment of the analogical world-view, but its consequence. If there is a connection between God and creation, if God's Word is truly made flesh in Christ, then the conversation and encounter between gospel and culture is a Christian imperative. Indeed, it is a condition for Christianity to come into being at all.

With this in mind, I would like to offer some very brief suggestions as to how Christian theology, learning from Radical Orthodoxy, can avoid its insularity.[30] Language, Community and Desire have been the three keynotes which have guided our discussion, and it is with these that we conclude.

Language in dialogue

The Christian Word is always in relationship, and always facing and engaging with a world that is not a part of God. Our ordinary human language, as Radical Orthodoxy suggests, can teach us much about the nature of God, but only if we avoid the idealism which cuts the lines of communication between languages.

I am spoken into being. Languages always come before me, and it is through signs that any identity I have is developed and secured. But identity is never final and fixed, as language is always open to newness. It is always, from the beginning, in dialogue.

In some ways, Radical Orthodoxy is ready to acknowledge this. Catherine Pickstock's bold claims about the way in which the Eucharist anchors the meaning of all signs can be looked at from another direction: the celebration of the sacramental depth potentially present in all language. If, as she argues, all signs are 'concelebration' (a sharing in the transforming blessing of the Eucharist, see p. 70 above), then our ordinary human use and abuse of language can have much to teach us about the way in which God is present in the world. Language connects worldly, material reality with shifting patterns of cultural meaning, whilst opening both matter and culture to a transcendent reality. Our ideas of what sacraments are will be shaped by this ordinary experience of communication. They bring a dialogue with worldliness into the heart of the Church's holiest of mysteries.

This sacramental dialogue is far from the oppressive, Eurocentric charade that Milbank rightly dismisses. It is a living encounter of particular others, and it involves the difficult ethical tasks of attention, translation, empathy and solidarity. It must be open to conversion, not simply a rehearsal of preconceived opinions. Radical Orthodoxy seeks to make space for the newness of God's word to speak to us, but it is so concerned to constrain this speaking within the limits of its idealized Church that it makes itself incapable of attending to other voices.

Such dialogue will never be free of cultural prejudices, but nor need it be a slave to narrow secularism. The very values it espouses are critical and self-critical. It can expose and challenge all that stands in the way of dialogue, all that denies people a voice. Among these barriers, as Radical Orthodoxy rightly points out, is that of the dogmatic anti-religious attitude best exemplified by contemporary figures such as Richard Dawkins, the Oxford scientist who dismisses God as delusion and faith as the opposite of thinking. True dialogue calls such self-enclosed views into question.

Ultimately, dialogue is true to the impulse of Christian faith, reflecting and enacting the communicative excess and freedom of creation, incarnation and Trinity. In the very act of creation, God forms an other, a being who cannot simply be reabsorbed into the divine without losing its integrity, its texture, its God-given depth and voice. Radical Orthodoxy is right to reaffirm that creation finds its depth only in relation to God's ever-renewed gift of being. In Christian terms, dialogue must become trialogue, a dynamic reality which always overflows the dogmatism of fundamentalists, whether secular or religious. But this also means that the Church can never rest secure that it can narrate these realities perfectly, or that it has nothing more to learn from new and strange accents. It is always open to learning the inexhaustible meaning of creation from those who have experienced it in different skins.

Community in compassion

The Christian God is made up of relationships, and the giving and receiving of love. Compassion is not alien to the Trinity. And the fact of the world, of there being something which is not God, invites us to imagine how God enjoys and suffers creation.

Radical Orthodoxy is right to warn us against the constant temptation to project all-too-human ideas of existence and relationship on to God. If God becomes nothing more than the reflection of our own insecurities and desires, then God is little more than an idol. However, this does not mean that classical ideas of God's self-sufficiency and immunity from change and suffering can simply be allowed to pass without challenge. It is ironic that a theology which sets so much store by theology's ability to take over all of philosophy's functions should still be so under the spell of Plato and the Greeks.

It is important to ask what difference creation, sin, history, incarnation and resurrection make to God, even if we are aware that our words are broken and fumbling. The God of the Bible and Christian tradition longs for his beloved, is grieved by sin. Through Christ, God takes on himself the vulnerability of the servant and is exposed to the reality of death. The Spirit is sent to be an ongoing guide for the Church in its geographical, historical and cultural journeying. In other words, God doesn't remain confined within the borders of our definitions of what is appropriate to the divine, any more than the father of the prodigal son bowed to the dictates of convention when running to meet his lost offspring on the road (Luke 15.20), or Jesus kept himself separate from the dirt, pain and celebration of human life. The scriptural stories do not offer a metaphysical blueprint of God, but they must inform a Christian understanding of God's nature. Perhaps one of the great weaknesses of Radical Orthodoxy is its inattention to this biblical challenge.

The Christian community that is formed in response to this revelation is called to embody a living compassion for and solidarity with creation. If it works towards mutuality and reconciliation between its members, it cannot turn its back on the world.

As Ward suggests, it must always risk itself beyond its borders. That risk entails the possibility that it will have to learn its own wounds, how it has caused violence to and received grace from others. Radical Orthodoxy is too ready to gloss over the ambiguities and failings of the premodern Church, and so has not done enough to convince its feminist and liberationist critics that it really has learnt the lessons of imperialism and patriarchy. A discipline of compassion might prevent us from rushing in to categorize people and tell their story for them, and free us to learn new lessons about how deep and wide the freedom of the gospel runs. Radical Orthodoxy itself has proved capable of moving beyond the established traditions of the Church to open up a more inclusive stance towards same-sex unions. Perhaps it needs to reflect upon what has motivated this move – one likely to make it deeply unpopular in conservative Christian quarters.

Compassion is therefore not a weak masochism, but a mature, confident humility. It does not wish away the realities of human mortality and fear with speculative doctrines, but lives with and learns from them. An ethic of compassion does not mean applying sticking plaster to the world's pains, but entering into them creatively, discerning the power of resurrection to transform lives and situations. However, to proclaim resurrection cannot mean to bypass the passion and cross, and the silence of the tomb.

Desire and unknowing

'What do I love, when I love my God?' St Augustine's question has been taken up by John Caputo, who argues that the question must always retain its note of uncertainty if it is to keep faith alive. If ever we claim to know who God is in an absolute and final way, faith will die. We will be left with an idol.[31]

One of the most striking aspects of many Radical Orthodox texts is their confidence. In some respects, this is quite justified. Theology need not be cowed by secularist assumptions about the privatization, irrationality and inevitable decline of religion. It can affirm that truth and reason are richer than Richard Dawkins and his allies suppose, and offer its own critique of the arrogance of violence hidden under secular facades.

Nevertheless, Radical Orthodoxy's self-assurance needs to be tempered by its own conviction that all our knowing and speaking is contextual. Interpretation is unavoidable, which makes it all the more frustrating that many of the authors we have discussed still seem to fantasize about moments of pure, immediate certainty and fusion with God.

In contrast with such conviction, agnosticism might seem to be a negative state of mind – an inability to decide, an uncertainty which paralyses us, or just plain laziness which can't be bothered to commit. However, it can be read in a very different way, touching on deep roots of Christian mysticism and the Jewish ban on images of God. It can seize on those moments when something of the emptiness, the void, opens up beneath all our cultural constructions and assured identities. And this experience (or quality of all our experiences) can be one of grace.

The 'negative' way in Christianity is a critical one; it exposes the limitations of all our images of God. In some versions, it can seem to promise a final wordless fusion with the divine. But it can also have a powerfully motivating effect. It arouses our desire, which, in Christian terms, should not seek to 'fix' and possess its object as another commodity to be used and domesticated or thrown away. There is always more to God than eye can see (or tongue can taste).

Is this just an otherworldly theology which cuts God off from the world? Not necessarily. The forms and sacraments in which God is met are real. But they are also fragile, vulnerable and limited. The God who is compassion, the Word in dialogue with flesh, establishes a true relationship with the world, without becoming identical with any part of it, or causing creation to lose its freedom and integrity.

In the moment of creation, the Word is spoken into a void or chaos of possibility. In a sense, for all the ordered nature of scientific law, the probabilities of evolution and the shaping lure of providence, there is no knowing what may come to pass. There is a proper freedom for creation to grow into what it may be. In Israel's covenant with God, the security and responsibility is set in a context of hostility to idols, and to gods which are simply identified with aspects of nature. The experiences of exodus and exile shape the biblical spirit, preparing us for the fact that all our most cherished identities and structures can collapse.

In Jesus' ministry, the question of his identity is always tantalizingly out of reach. The sense of being called to follow, without knowing the end of the road, is palpable. It reaches its most intense pitch in Jesus' own cry of desolation from the cross. But it is not ended by the resurrection, as the disciples continue to struggle even to recognize a Jesus who always eludes their grasp. And when the Spirit is sent on the Church, none can guess the truth into which it will lead them, or the strange and alien voices through which the Church will receive the Spirit afresh from outside its boundaries.

The path of unknowing is thus not mere self-indulgent abstraction. It can free us from the speculative drive to identify God with our own partial constructions. But its role is more than critical. It is also a liberation to enjoy the mystery of God and the mystery of creation, to let them be what they are. The gift is always mediated, never 'pure'. But it creates a space in which our being might be open to a value and a presence which cannot be calculated.

Dialogue, Compassion and Unknowing might be the three marks of a theology to come, because they are also ancient and woven into the texts of Christian theology and the textures of Christian experience. They are mystical and everyday, personal and political, open to the world and yet critical of its idolatries and superficiality. They are both radical and orthodox, but in a sense that troubles the settled meaning of those terms. Perhaps Radical Orthodoxy's gift to us is this: the strangeness of its adopted title, whose tensions can never be resolved, signals the coming of a strange God, an Other for our wondering.

Chapter summary

Four areas have been identified in which Radical Orthodoxy has been subjected to criticism:

- *Dualism.* It is argued that Radical Orthodoxy traps Christian theology and the Church into a separate sphere, cut off from the world and other discourses. Some even claim that this theology is guilty of a Gnostic tendency to divide the world up into pure good and pure evil. This is a travesty of the Christian doctrine of creation, and it condemns theology to talk only to itself.
- *Imperialism.* Despite its rejection of western liberalism, Radical Orthodoxy is charged with its own will to domination. It risks imposing an idealized view of the Church and theology on others, claiming all truth for itself. Its image of God excludes any sense that God can really experience the ambiguity and suffering of the world, and so has no place for the victims of worldly injustice.
- *Rootlessness.* Radical Orthodoxy's view of the Church is heavily criticized by those who see it as an unreal, ahistorical projection, which glosses over the messy reality of church history and division. Some argue that Christ is also made into a mere metaphor or a piece of speculative poetry. Material, embodied creation and history are emptied of their significance.
- *Monism.* For some critics, the final aim of Radical Orthodoxy is to overwhelm and absorb all alternative positions. Theologically, it is suspected of using doctrines like participation and transubstantiation to deny the ultimate distinction between God and creation, as it seeks a moment of pure fusion with the divine.

Some of these criticisms fail to take into account some of the subtleties of Radical Orthodoxy's own positions, but they cannot all be shaken off. We have noted, however, that Radical Orthodoxy itself is diverse, and that Graham Ward in particular has suggested a way forward involving more awareness of other perspectives and of the limits of our knowledge.

Finally, we have explored the outlines of an alternative theological approach which learns from Radical Orthodoxy but challenges its dogmatism. It has been tackled under three headings:

- *Language in dialogue.* All our communication is dialogical, opening us to the Other. This is rooted in a Christian view of creation, incarnation and sacraments.

- *Community in compassion.* The Christian community is shaped by God's compassionate giving of life to the world, and should not be turned in on itself.
- *Desire and unknowing.* Agnosticism is part of Christian faith's inner dynamic and its experience of a God who cannot be contained in any single perspective, story or image.

Notes

Introduction: insider theology?

1 Stephen Long, 'Radical Orthodoxy' in Kevin Vanhoozer (ed.), *The Cambridge Companion to Postmodern Theology*, Cambridge University Press, Cambridge, 2003, p. 133.

2 See for example *TST*, pp. 302–3; *WMS*, pp. 41–9; *TA*, p. 33; *AW*, pp. 21–140; *LTEH*, pp. 13–14; *DE*, pp. 167–8; *PSP*, pp. 6–7; Conor Cunningham, *Genealogy of Nihilism*, Routledge, London, 2002, pp. 27–8. For a critique, see Richard Cross in *DRO*, pp. 65–80.

3 Milbank is discussing the arguments of René Girard in this passage.

4 John Milbank, *The Suspended Middle: Henri de Lubac and the Debate Concerning the Supernatural*, Eerdmans, Grand Rapids, 2005, pp. ix–x.

5 Tracey Rowland, *Culture and the Thomist Tradition*, Routledge, London, pp. 159–61.

6 See Alasdair MacIntyre, *After Virtue*, University of Notre Dame Press, Notre Dame, 1984; *Whose Justice? Which Rationality?* University of Notre Dame Press, Notre Dame, 1988; *Three Rival Versions of Moral Enquiry: Encyclopedia, Genealogy and Tradition*, University of Notre Dame Press, Notre Dame, 1990.

7 See Stanley Hauerwas, *The Peaceable Kingdom: A Primer in Christian Ethics*, University of Notre Dame Press, Notre Dame, 1983; John Berkman and Michael Cartwright (eds), *The Hauerwas Reader*, Duke University Press, Durham and London, 2001.

8 George Lindbeck, *The Nature of Doctrine: Religion and Theology in a Postliberal Age*, London, SPCK, 1984.

9 James K. A. Smith, *Introducing Radical Orthodoxy: Mapping a Post-Secular Theology*, Baker Academic, Grand Rapids, 2004, pp. 257–8.

1 Language: telling God's story

1 Søren Kierkegaard, *Either/Or Part One*, Princeton University Press, Princeton, 1987, p. 30.

2 Kierkegaard, *Either/Or Part One*, p. 32.

3 See Ludwig Wittgenstein, *Philosophical Investigations*, Blackwell, Oxford, 1958.

4 Don Cupitt, *The Long Legged Fly*, SCM Press, London, 1987, p. 13.

5 Graham Ward, *Barth, Derrida and the Language of Theology*, Cambridge University Press, Cambridge, 1995, p. 9.

6 John Milbank, 'Postmodern Critical Augustinianism: A Short Summa in Forty-Two Responses to Unasked Questions', *Modern Theology*, 1991, p. 225.

7 Gerard Loughlin, *Telling God's Story: Bible, Church and Narrative Theology*, Cambridge University Press, Cambridge, 1996.

8 It should be noted that Milbank says that 'perhaps Judaism' also affirms ultimate peace (*TST*, p. 262).

9 Ward, *Barth, Derrida and the Language of Theology*, p. 248.

2 Community: the all-consuming Church

1 John Berkman and Michael Cartwright (eds), *The Hauerwas Reader*, Duke University Press, Durham and London, 2001, p. 219.

2 William Cavanaugh, *Torture and Eucharist: Theology, Politics and the Body of Christ*, Blackwell, Oxford, 1998.

3 John Milbank, 'Postmodern Critical Augustinianism: A Short Summon in Forty-Two Responses to Unasked Questions', *Modern Theology*, 1991, p. 228.

4 See Jacques Derrida, *Given Time 1: Counterfeit Money*, University of Chicago Press, Chicago, 1992; *The Gift of Death*, University of Chicago Press, Chicago, 1995.

5 Gavin D'Costa, 'Seeking after Theological Vision', *Reviews in Religion and Theology* 6.4, 1999, p. 356.

6 John Milbank, 'Enclaves, or Where is the Church?' *New Blackfriars* 73, 1992, p. 342.

7 See *WMS*, p. 162; *TST*, pp. 383–4; Milbank, 'Postmodern Critical Augustinianism', p. 232.

8 Milbank, 'Postmodern Critical Augustinianism', p. 229.

9 James K. A. Smith, *Introducing Radical Orthodoxy: Mapping a Post Secular Theology*, Baker Academic, Grand Rapids, 2004, p. 243n.

10 Smith, *Introducing Radical Orthodoxy*, p. 257 and p. 257n.

3 Desire: what we really want

1 For further explorations of the idea of non-identical repetition, see also *TST*, pp. 211–14 and *PSP*, p. 132.

2 Elizabeth Stuart, *Gay and Lesbian Theologies. Repetitions with Critical Difference*, Ashgate, Aldershot, 2003, p. 106.

3 Stuart, *Gay and Lesbian Theologies*, p. 108.

4 Stuart, *Gay and Lesbian Theologies*, p. 108.

5 Stephen Long, *The Goodness of God: Theology, Church and Social Order*, Brazos Press, Grand Rapids, 2001.

6 See Steven Shakespeare, 'The New Romantics: A Critique of Radical Orthodoxy', *Theology* 103.813, 2000, pp. 163–77.

4 Looking ahead: (not) knowing the end of the story

 1 Paul O'Grady, 'Anti-Foundationalism and Radical Orthodoxy', *New Blackfriars* 81, 2000, p. 175.

 2 Richard Roberts, 'Transcendental Sociology? A Critique of John Milbank's *Theology and Social Theory. Beyond Secular Reason*', *Scottish Journal of Theology* 46.4, 1993, p. 535.

 3 Aidan Nichols, ' "Non tali auxilio": John Milbank's Suasion to Orthodoxy', *New Blackfriars* 73, 1992, p. 327.

 4 See Douglas Hedley, 'Should Divinity Overcome Metaphysics? Reflections on John Milbank's "Theology Beyond Secular Reason" and "Confessions of a Cambridge Platonist" ', *The Journal of Religion* 80, 2000, pp. 271–98; Paul Janz, 'Radical Orthodoxy and the New Culture of Obscurantism', *Modern Theology* 20.3, 2004, pp. 363–405.

 5 Janz, 'Obscurantism', p. 399.

 6 Gavin Hyman, *The Predicament of Postmodern Theology: Radical Orthodoxy or Nihilist Textualism?* Westminster John Knox Press, Louisville, 2001, p. 70.

 7 Jeffrey Stout, *Democracy and Tradition*, Princeton University Press, Princeton, 2004, p. 93.

 8 Stout, *Democracy and Tradition*, p. 115.

 9 Rowan Williams, 'Saving Time: Thoughts on Practice, Patience and Vision', *New Blackfriars* 73, 1992, p. 323.

10 Roberts, 'Transcendental Sociology?', p. 533; Theo Hobson, 'Rethinking Postmodern Theology' *Modern Believing* 47.3, 2006, p. 11; *ITP*, p. 110.

11 Williams, 'Saving Time', p. 323.

12 Debra Dean Murphy, 'Power, Politics and Difference: A Feminist Response to John Milbank', *Modern Theology* 10.2, 2004, p. 136.

13 Mark Chapman, review of *LTEH*, *The Journal of Theological Studies* 54.2, 2003, p. 857.

14 Hyman, *The Predicament of Postmodern Theology*, p. 73.

15 Gavin D'Costa, 'Seeking after Theological Vision', *Reviews in Religion and Theology* 6.4, 1999, p. 358.

16 Nichols, 'Non tali auxilio', p. 330.

17 See George Pattison's comments in *DRO*, pp. 149–60.

18 Ross Thompson, 'Postmodernism and the "Trinity": How to be Postmodern and Post-Barthian too', *New Blackfriars* 83, 2002, p. 175.

19 R. R. Reno, 'The Radical Orthodoxy Project', *First Things* 100, 2000, p. 42.

20 Mark C. Mattes, 'A Lutheran Assessment of Radical Orthodoxy', *Lutheran Quarterly* 15.3, 2001, p. 40.

21 Simon Taylor, 'Keep Taking the Medicine: Radical Orthodoxy and the Future of Theology', *Modern Believing* 41.4, 2000, p. 40.

22 Frederick Bauerschmidt, 'The Word Made Speculative? John Milbank's Christological Poetics', *Modern Theology* 15, 1999, pp. 417–32.

23 Hyman, *The Predicament of Postmodern Theology*, p. 77.

24 Hyman, *The Predicament of Postmodern Theology*, p. 85.

25 Søren Kierkegaard, *Either/Or Part One*, Princeton University Press, Princeton, 1987, p. 19.

26 Graham Ward, 'John Milbank's Divina Commedia', *New Blackfriars* 73, 1992, p. 316.

27 Ward, 'John Milbank's Divina Commedia', p. 315.

28 Graham Ward, *Christ and Culture*, Blackwell, Oxford, 2005, p. 14.

29 Ward, *Christ and Culture*, p. 15.

30 Some works I have found helpful are George Pattison, *Agnosis: Theology in the Void*, Macmillan, Basingstoke and London, 1996, and *The End of Theology and the Task of Thinking About God*, SCM Press, London, 1998; Gordon Kaufman, *In Face of Mystery: A Constructive Theology*, Cambridge MA and London, 1993; Peter Rollins, *How (Not) to Speak of God*, SPCK, London, 2006; Oliver Davies, *A Theology of Compassion*, SCM Press, London, 2001.

31 John Caputo, *On Religion*, Routledge, London, 2001.

Further reading

Bibliographical resource

For those undertaking more detailed research, a full, updated bibliography of works connected with Radical Orthodoxy can be found at 'Radical Orthodoxy Online', at <www.calvin.edu/%7Ejks4/ro/robib.pdf>

The 'Radical Orthodoxy' series of books

Bell, D., *Liberation Theology after the End of History: The Refusal to Cease Suffering*, Routledge, London, 2001.

Cunningham, C., *Genealogy of Nihilism*, Routledge, London, 2002.

Hanby, M., *Augustine and Modernity*, Routledge, London, 2003.

Long, S., *Divine Economy: Theology and the Market*, Routledge, London, 2000.

Milbank, J., *Being Reconciled: Ontology and Pardon*, Routledge, London, 2003.

Milbank, J. and Pickstock, C., *Truth in Aquinas*, Routledge, London, 2001.

Milbank, J., Pickstock, C. and Ward, G. (eds), *Radical Orthodoxy: A New Theology*, Routledge, London, 1999.

Miner, R., *Truth in the Making: Knowledge and Creation in Modern Philosophy and Theology*, Routledge, London, 2003.

Oliver, S., *Philosophy, God and Motion*, Routledge, London, 2005.

Rowland, T., *Culture and the Thomist Tradition: After Vatican II*, Routledge, London, 2003.

Smith, J., *Speech and Theology: The Language and Logic of Incarnation*, Routledge, London, 2002.

Ward, G., *Cities of God*, Routledge, London, 2000.

Additional selected major works by Radical Orthodox theologians

Blond, P. (ed.), *Post-Secular Philosophy: Between Philosophy and Theology*, Routledge, London, 1998.

Cavanaugh, W., *Torture and Eucharist: Theology, Politics and the Body of Christ*, Blackwell, Oxford, 1998.

Loughlin, G., *Telling God's Story: Bible, Church and Narrative Theology*, Cambridge University Press, Cambridge, 1996.

Milbank, J., *Theology and Social Theory: Beyond Secular Reason*, Blackwell, Oxford, 1990 (2nd edn 2006).

Milbank, J., *The Word Made Strange: Theology, Language, Culture*, Blackwell, Oxford, 1997.

Pickstock, C., *After Writing: On the Liturgical Consummation of Philosophy*, Blackwell, Oxford, 1998.

Smith, J., *Introducing Radical Orthodoxy: Mapping a Post-Secular Theology*, Baker Academic, Grand Rapids, 2004.

Ward, G., *Christ and Culture*, Blackwell, Oxford, 2005.

Ward, G., *Cultural Transformation and Religious Practice*, Cambridge University Press, Cambridge, 2005.

Dialogue, commentary and critique

Hankey, W. and Hedley, D. (eds), *Deconstructing Radical Orthodoxy: Postmodern Theology, Rhetoric and Truth*, Ashgate, Aldershot, 2005.

Hemming, L. (ed.), *Radical Orthodoxy? A Catholic Enquiry*, Ashgate, Aldershot, 2000.

Hyman, G., *The Predicament of Postmodern Theology: Radical Orthodoxy or Nihilist Textualism?*, Westminster John Knox Press, Louisville, 2001.

Radford Ruether, R. and Grau, M. (eds), *Interpreting the Postmodern: Responses to 'Radical Orthodoxy'*, T & T Clark, New York and London, 2006.

Smith, J. and Olthius, J. (eds), *Radical Orthodoxy and the Reformed Tradition: Creation, Covenant and Participation*, Baker Academic, Grand Rapids, 2005.

Full details of other books and articles quoted in the text can be found in the relevant notes.

Index

The SPCK Introduction to Karl Rahner
Karen Kilby
(ISBN: 978 0 281 05842 6)

'Karen Kilby's book will be invaluable to teachers and students because of its lucid, learned, and penetrating understanding of one of the most important theologians of the twentieth century. It is the best single slim volume on Rahner that I know.'
Gavin D'Costa, University of Bristol

'Karen Kilby's book is an imaginative, clear and succinct work. It offers many illustrative and accessible analogies which I have found invaluable in communicating important aspects of Rahner's thought to students.'
Philip Caldwell, Ushaw College, Durham

'I have never come across a more useful tool in presenting Rahner to undergraduates than Kilby's book. It is a model of succinctness and precision, but far more importantly, it succeeds in accurately identifying and unpacking the key to Rahner's thought in a very reader-friendly way.'
Eamonn Mulcahy, Missionary Institute, London

'Lucid, perceptive, thickly textured, theologically rich, and refreshingly concise – Kilby's presentation of Rahner's theology is a must for students of Rahner, be they first year seminarians or senior theologians. I have taught her book for years and I still learn something new from it every time I return – it's brilliant reading.'
Serene Jones, Yale Divinity School

'This is an excellent book, very useful for students and one of the clearest introductions to Rahner.'
John McDade, Principal of Heythrop College, London

Karen Kilby is an Associate Professor in the Department of Theology and Religious Studies at the University of Nottingham. She is the author of *Karl Rahner: Theology and Practice*.

The SPCK Introduction to Simone Weil
Stephen Plant
(ISBN: 978 0 281 05938 6)

'This is a lucid and readable introduction to one of the twentieth century's most fascinating religious thinkers. Stephen Plant guides his readers through key themes in Simone Weil's work, raising important questions as he goes. This is invaluable reading for students and teachers alike.'

Nicholas Sagovsky, Canon Theologian of Westminster Abbey

'Stephen Plant commends Simone Weil's voice as distinctive and important in the conversation that is Christian theological reflection. She provokes us to serious concern about justice, the goals of politics, and the characteristics of our societies. Her attempts to discern the presence of God in the most profound human distress make her worth reading and rereading. Stephen Plant is an illuminating guide to her passionate quest for truth and truthfulness.'

**Ann Loades CBE, Professor Emerita of
Divinity University of Durham**

'A wonderfully concise and sensitive portrayal of Simone Weil's thought and religion, enriched by the many quotations from her own writings.'

The Expository Times

'Simone Weil's life and writings remain both fruitful and troubling for Christian thought. This elegant, thorough and accessible introduction enables readers to encounter Weil and to confront the compelling questions she raises.'

Dr Rachel Muers, University of Leeds

Stephen Plant is Senior Tutor and Director of Studies at Wesley House in the Cambridge Theological Federation and an affiliated lecturer in the University of Cambridge. He is the author of *Bonhoeffer*.

Thomas, the Other Gospel
Nicholas Perrin
(ISBN: 978 0 281 05871 6)

'The *Gospel of Thomas* has been at the centre of a great deal of recent speculation about Christian Origins, but few people actually know what it is, and what is in it. Nicholas Perrin is at the cutting edge of serious *Thomas* scholarship, and this book makes accessible to a wider audience his brilliant reconstruction of how the document came to be written, what it meant then, and what it means now.'

Tom Wright, Bishop of Durham

'This book challenges the notion that *Thomas* is as old as the New Testament Gospels and contains independent and perhaps even superior Jesus tradition . . . must reading for anyone who wants to know the truth about the *Gospel of Thomas*.'

Craig A. Evans, Payzant Distinguished Professor of New Testament Acadia Divinity College

'Here we have judicious scholarship from an expert in *Thomas* that demands a reassessment of the current state of research on *Thomas*, its dating, and its place in the development of early Christianity.'

Marianne Meye Thompson, Professor of New Testament Interpretation Fuller Theological Seminary

'Perrin offers a new, provocative hypothesis . . . a very readable book with much valuable information and many fresh insights.'

Jens Schröter, Professor of New Testament University of Leipzig

'[A] well-written, thought-provoking examination of current scholarship on the *Gospel of Thomas* . . . must reading for students of the New Testament and early church history, indeed for all those who care about who Jesus is for us today.'

Robert Van Voorst, Professor of New Testament Western Theological Seminary

'Delightful to read . . . a stunning achievement that can set the standard for the next generation of scholarship.'

Scot McKnight, Karl A. Olsson Professor in Religious Studies North Park University

Nicholas Perrin is Assistant Professor of New Testament at Wheaton College Graduate School, Illinois. He is the author of *Thomas and Tatian: The Relationship between the* Diatessaron *and the* Gospel of Thomas and is the joint editor of *Questioning Q.*